JUV
HC
255
.B596
1995

Bland, Celia.

The mechanical age.

$17.95

DATE			

WORLD HISTORY LIBRARY

THE
MECHANICAL AGE

The Industrial Revolution in England

CELIA BLAND

Facts On File®

AN INFOBASE HOLDINGS COMPANY

The author would like to gratefully acknowledge the assistance of Alexander Zane, Leigh Hope Wood, Eddie Miu, and Anthony and Eusie Zane in completing this book.

On the cover: The Great Eastern: Isambard Kingdom
Brunel Inspecting Checking Drum, Nov. 1857, photo by Robert Howlett.

The Mechanical Age: The Industrial Revolution

Facts On File, Inc.
460 Park Avenue South
New York, NY 10016

Library of Congress Cataloging-in-Publication Data
Bland, Celia.
   The mechanical age : the industrial revolution in England / Celia
Bland.
      p. cm. — (World history library)
   Includes bibliographical references and index.
   Summary: Surveys the social and mechanical innovations of the
Industrial Revolution in England and the reforms and imperialism
that grew out of these changes.
   ISBN 0-8160-3139-8
   1. Industrial revolution—England—History—Juvenile literature.
2. England—Social conditions—Juvenile literature.   [1. Industrial
revolution—England. 2. England—Social conditions—18th century.
3. England—Social conditions—19th century.] I. Title.   II. Series.
HC255.B596 1995
338.0941—dc20   94-40971

Facts On File books are available at special discounts when purchased in bulk quantities for businesses, associations, institutions or sales promotions. Please call our Special Sales Department in New York at 212/683-2244 or 800/322-8755.

Text design by Donna Sinisgalli
Cover design by Amy Gonzalez
Maps by Florence Neal
This book is printed on acid-free paper.

Printed in the United States of America
MP FOF 10 9 8 7 6 5 4 3 2 1

CONTENTS

*Were we required to characterize this age of ours
by any single epithet, we should be tempted to
call it . . . the Mechanical Age.*

—Thomas Carlyle
Signs of the Times, 1829

A NOTE ON BRITISH MONEY

During the 18th and 19th centuries, a pound sterling (£) was made up of 240 silver pennies. A shilling equaled 12 pennies. Halfpennies and farthings equaled one-quarter of a penny. A guinea was a gold coin worth 21 shillings. A sovereign was a gold pound. Bank notes were first issued in the latter half of the 17th century; in the 19th century the Bank of England was given a monopoly on issuing notes. In 1971, Britain shifted to a decimal currency, and the pound and pence were based on units of 10, just as the dollar is in the United States.

The average man working in a factory earned between £8 and £9 a year in 1700, £12 and £13 in 1750, £22 in 1800, and £44 in 1860. The average working woman made anywhere from a fourth to three-fourths of these yearly amounts, depending upon her trade.

The British Isles

SCOTLAND

Atlantic
Ocean

North
Sea

Glasgow
Edinburgh

NORTH-
UMBERLAND

Newcastle

Belfast

York

Leeds

Manchester

Liverpool LANCASHIRE Sheffield

Mersey R. Nottingham

Dublin

CHESHIRE

Derby

THE MIDLANDS

Shannon River

IRELAND

Birmingham

ENGLAND

WALES

Cardiff Oxford London

Thames R.

Southampton Portsmouth

CORNWALL Plymouth

English Channel

FRANCE

N

0   100 mi

0   100 km

THE
INDUSTRIAL
SPIRIT

In 1776, the same year that American colonists declared their independence from British rule, a near-sighted, notoriously absent-minded Scotsman published a book called *An Inquiry into the Nature and Causes of the Wealth of Nations.* Setting down the guidelines for another revolution—an industrial revolution—in 1,000 pages of closely argued text, Dr. Adam Smith described an economy moving from agriculture to mechanization. *The Wealth of Nations* has been called "the prescription for the spectacles of generations."

England in Adam Smith's time was a country of farmers, merchants, and shepherds. Aristocrats owned most of the arable land, and their comfortable houses and stables were maintained by the rents they charged to farmers for the use of that land. In the cities and towns, shopkeepers sold little more than hand-knit socks, woolens, furniture, plow bits, and a few articles imported from France and Holland, a situation that seemed unlikely to change because Parliament, England's governing body, limited international trade by legislating tariffs (taxes) on foreign goods.

ADAM SMITH (1723-90)

Few philosophers have had such unlucky beginnings as Adam Smith. When only four years old he was stolen by Gypsies. His father had died six months before his birth, and it was Smith's uncle who pursued the Gypsy band, recovering the boy and returning him to his doting mother. Young Adam grew up to become a brilliant scholar, as famous for his eccentric behavior as for his inquisitive mind. A friend recounts a walk with Smith during which the distracted philosopher fell into a pit. Another time, Smith left his house in his nightgown and, lost in a reverie, walked 15 miles before "coming to." He was famous for carrying on dialogues with himself, arguing theoretical questions as he paced the cobblestone streets of Edinburgh.

In 1759 Smith published *The Theory of Moral Sentiments*, a consideration of the motives of self-interest and impartiality in society, and his reputation as a man of intellect was made. Already a professor of logic at Glasgow University in Scotland, he was engaged as the tutor of the young duke of Buccleuch in 1764 and traveled the capitals of Europe for two years with his youthful charge. In Paris and London, Smith discussed ideas with the great minds of his day—Voltaire, David Hume, and Benjamin Franklin—while writing the treatise that would become his masterpiece.

Published in 1776, *The Wealth of Nations* was a best-seller. Its simple, even homely style translated complex economic theories

England's neighbors—Scotland, Wales, and Ireland—were even more provincial. In Kirkcaldy, the village where Adam Smith was born, iron nails rather than minted coins were used as currency. In Cornwall, a peninsula in southwestern England, men mined tin as they had for centuries, lowering themselves by ropes into small holes in the earth, where they loosened the ore with pickaxes. It was understood that working alone in the dark, miners often slept as many hours as they labored.

into a language that could be understood by the average citizen. Described as "the outpouring not only of a great mind, but of a whole epoch," *The Wealth of Nations* is a panoramic look at society, touching upon everything from ancient African kingdoms to the projected profits of keeping an alehouse. Translated into Danish, French, German, Italian, and Spanish, *The Wealth of Nations* was often quoted in parliamentary debates by both liberal and conservative speakers. So respected did Smith become that when he was invited to meet Prime Minister William Pitt at a congress of the most influential statesmen of the age, the assembled legislators rose to their feet as he entered the room. "Be seated, gentlemen," the Scotsman pleaded. "No," replied Pitt, "we will stand until you are first seated, for we are all your scholars."

Smith ended his life putting his economic theories to the test as the commissioner of customs in Edinburgh. He died at the age of 67, and his dying wish that all 16 volumes of his manuscripts be burned was carried out. Friends destroyed what may have been an even greater work than *The Wealth of Nations*, a manuscript outlining a theory of government that the philosopher had been formulating for more than a decade.

The historian Robert Heilbroner describes Smith as the first philosopher to concern himself with humanity's desire for wealth; in today's terms, Smith was the world's first economist. Smith himself never believed that his ideas were revolutionary. As Heilbroner says, Smith was only giving "the world the image of itself for which it had been searching."

Britain was ripe for change and, due to certain advantages, its progress from an agricultural backwater to an industrial power would be rapid. First, England's banking system and credit facilities were more flexible than those of its European counterparts, and the nation's many prosperous merchants and landowners were, for a variety of reasons, willing to finance new enterprises. Second, Britain's navy was the greatest in the world, giving England ready access to the natural resources of other countries, as well as the means to transport its own manufactured goods to foreign markets. Finally, and most importantly, English, Irish, Welsh, and Scottish men and women formed a large and eager workforce that was desperate for employment, one result of sweeping political and economic changes in the late 17th century.

Revolution implies a sudden and violent change, but the period known as the Industrial Revolution in fact encompassed a series of gradual, evolutionary developments. Historians debate both the actual dates of the Industrial Revolution in England—some believe it ran from 1714–1815, others from 1760–1830, or from 1765–1880—and whether several Industrial Revolutions occurred, or just one with different phases. But all agree that the Industrial Revolution was a period when the British began to look forward and to experiment with new ways of doing things. Not bloody like its cousins the American and the French Revolutions, the Industrial Revolution nonetheless would be fought by those who resisted the progress of mechanization and capitalism, and those who made fortunes from the goods and products made possible by that revolution. This book covers the social and mechanical innovations of the Industrial Revolution itself, as well two offshoots of that revolution: industrial and social reforms and imperialism.

AGRICULTURE

The Industrial Revolution was helped along by some early innovations in agriculture. In 1731, a gentleman farmer named Jethro Tull published *Horse-hoeing Husbandry*, a manual advising farmers to alter the way they planted their crops.

Traditionally, a sower had ambled through his fields, casting his seeds upon the ground. Many seeds were washed away by rain or eaten by birds or field mice, and only a small number actually took root. Tull invented a hollow drill that bored straight rows of holes into the ground into which seeds could be dropped. This new technique for planting greatly increased the yield of grain or vegetables from each field. Tull also invented the horse hoe, an implement that broke up the earth for more efficient irrigation.

Tull's modernizations were advocated by King George III—nicknamed "Farmer George" for his interest in agriculture—and they were gradually adopted throughout the country. The king established a model farm at his palace at Windsor and set the fashion for farming experiments. Soon came new theories of stock breeding and crop rotation (the planting of different crops in different seasons to prevent the depletion of nutrients in the soil), and the introduction of such new vegetables as turnips, artichokes, and asparagus. Visitors traveled from all over Europe to visit the "progressive" farm of the agricultural innovator Robert Bakewell, where they admired his horses, cattle, and the sheep he called "machines for turning grass into mutton."

Enclosures

As modern methods boosted the profits of farming, the possession of land brought new social prestige and, at times, increased political influence. Aristocrats scrambled to buy more land so they could have more farms to rent. These landowners might hold as many as 200 acres, but their plots were often separated by the fields and pastures of smaller farmers. With their newfound wealth, the "landed gentry," as these landowners were called, bought out the small farmers, leveled cottages and barns, and consolidated fields and pastures. Those gentlemen farmers who were members of parliament (MPs) supported a new law called the Enclosure Act, which allowed them to annex to their estates "waste lands"—the woods, pastures, and open fields that villagers and farming communities shared. Between 1760 and 1790, nearly 3 million acres of waste lands were enclosed in the Midlands (the middle counties of England) alone. Woods were cut down for timber, communal pastures plowed under, and the open fields planted with corn or wheat. These consolidated farms were easier to plow, plant, irrigate, and manage, and by 1813 England had increased its agricultural production by one-fourth.

Some, however, regretted the changes wrought upon England's countryside. Writing in 1826, the journalist William Cobbett criticized the dispossession of small farmers. He was horrified that one man could own "as one farm the lands that those now living remember to have formed fourteen farms. . . ." The most brutal cases of forcible enclosure were in Scotland, where as many as 10,000 farming families were violently driven from their cottages by the countess of Sutherland between the years 1807–21.

Modern agricultural methods brought a change in the standard of living for the newly prosperous landowners. Farmers who once had eaten with their field hands now "put on airs" and "aped their betters" (as Cobbett put it), mimicking as best they could the lifestyles of the aristocracy. They now educated their daughters as well as their sons, drove a carriage, and ate off Wedgewood china rather than pewter. Some sold their large farms to other landowners, invested in business, and made fortunes—which they then invested in farms. "It was a frequent complaint of eighteenth-century writers that business men of the towns were purchasing land and entering the ranks of the landed gentry," the historian W. T. Selley comments. "But once installed on a country estate the business man applied the energy and principles of commerce to agriculture: he set out to farm his land to its greatest possible advantage. . . ."

THE BIRTH OF THE FACTORY SYSTEM

These "principles of commerce" were the very laws for economic growth defined in *The Wealth of Nations*. Adam Smith was interested in the interrelation of the different elements of a country's economy and in the connections between its natural resources, laborers, products, and markets. He believed that a well-thought-out economic system would mean a continual accumulation of wealth for the poor as well as the rich. He recognized, however, that for many people the pursuit of wealth and power was an end in itself. "With the greater part of rich people," he wrote, "the chief enjoyment of riches consists in the parade of riches, which in their eye is never so complete as when they appear to possess those decisive marks of opulence which nobody can possess but themselves."

Smith asserted that one way to increase a society's wealth was to recognize that economics are based upon people working together to produce goods or perform services—in other words, upon the division of labor. "Just look at the possessions of an ordinary working man," Smith argued.

The man's coat has been produced as a complex result of the work of a shepherd, a wool-sorter, a wool-comber, a dyer, a spinner, a weaver, and so on. Then merchants and sailors have been involved in transporting some of the materials used by certain of these workers . . . how much commerce and navigation . . . how many ship-builders, sailors, sail-makers, rope makers . . . !

The coat would never have been made at all if one person in this elaborate linkage had failed to do his or her job. A country's economy, then, Smith argued, was an elaborate chain of cooperation. But this dependency owed little to selflessness or altruism. As Smith wryly put it:

> It is not from the benevolence of the butcher, the brewer, or the baker that we expect our dinner but from their regard to their self-interest. We address ourselves, not to their humanity, but to their self-love, and never talk to them of our necessities, but of their advantages.

In fact, the consumer and the supplier were exchanging self-interests; they were mutually dependent for services, goods, and money.

A new production technique known as the factory system, in which each worker performed a specific task in the production of a commodity, was revolutionizing British industry. In Smith's view, the factory system was a major step toward developing a thriving economy. Taking the manufacture of pins as an example, Smith described a new pin factory as a marvel of productivity:

> I have seen a small manufactory of this kind where ten men only were employed and where some of them consequently performed two or three distinct operations . . . they could, when they exerted themselves, make among them about twelve pounds of pins in a day. There are in a pound upwards of four thousand pins . . . if they had all wrought separately and independently . . . they certainly could not each of them make twenty, perhaps not one pin a day. . . .

But, asked Smith, what is the *real* price of these pins? The price of their production. What is the price the manufacturer will get for them? Whatever price consumers are willing to pay. Price is based upon what other pin manufacturers are asking for their wares, the availability of pins, and the quality of the product. The price of pins, in Smith's estimation, is thus determined by the consumer's buying power, not by government controls or restrictions, or by the cost of their manufacturing. He believed that the market should regulate itself. "For to what purpose is all the toil and bustle of the pursuit of wealth, or power, and pre-eminence," he asked, unless it furthered "natural liberty" (as he called commercial capitalism).

It follows that Smith was as opposed to tariffs and other price protection legislation—"governments are spendthrift, irresponsible, and unproductive"—as he was to manufacturing monopolies and price-fixing—"People of the same trade seldom meet together but the conversation ends in a conspiracy against the public, or in some diversion to raise prices." Such practices hindered the working of the market and lessened society's potential to create wealth.

As elementary as these ideas may seem today, in 1776 they were revolutionary. It was not many years before Smith's birth that medieval laws prohibiting merchants from reaping large profits or craftsmen from experimenting with mechanical innovations were abolished, nor was the pursuit of personal wealth rather than spiritual redemption acknowledged as an acceptable goal in life until the late 17th century. The transition from seeking spiritual rewards to seeking material "gaine" was, in Smith's eyes, epitomized by the attitudes and habits of the new *entrepreneurs,* or organizers, of the textile industry.

Entrepreneurs in the Textile Trade

An entrepreneur is, according to modern terminology, a middleman. In the late 18th century, entrepreneurs were changing the way cloth was manufactured. Formerly, a family might have raised sheep, which it sheared, spun the wool into thread, woven it into cloth, and sold or traded the cloth in a local market for money, goods, or services. The entrepreneur, using the new methods of dividing labor, bought wool from a sheep farmer. He paid spinners to spin thread, then took the thread to weavers who, working at large handlooms in their cottages, wove it into cloth. The entrepreneur then sold the cloth at a profit to merchants in the cities and towns.

In the wool trade, the entrepreneur's profits were often small, but after 1750 it became possible to reap large profits from the sale of cotton cloth as the commercial demand for cotton increased. Parliament had recently forbidden the import of cotton from India, and the English public's desire for light, colorful fabrics prompted entrepreneurs to find the means to produce them domestically. Soon the demand for cotton cloth was so great that entrepreneurs could not find enough spinners to fill the orders for thread, as "even old barns, cart-houses and outbuildings of any description were fitted up for loom-shops."

Unlike wool, cotton must be spun in a moist climate to prevent static electricity from creating knots and tangles in the thread. In England, only two areas—Cheshire and Lancashire—had the right climate for cotton spinning, but they were sparsely populated. When no new spinners could be found in these counties, entrepreneurs began to offer prizes for a machine that would spin cotton yarn.

In 1764, the invention of the "spinning jenny," a simple hand device that spun six or seven threads simultaneously, revolutionized the production of cotton thread. Two years later, Richard Arkwright took the jenny and improved upon it, inventing a "water frame." The water frame, however, was so large it would not fit into a cottage, and so heavy it needed mechanical power—a waterwheel—to run it. Thus the first cotton factory was built.

By 1774, Arkwright had two factories complete with water frames and two new water-powered looms, but he had no workforce. Local spinners and weavers worked their own hours in their own homes. Unused to wage labor, they valued their independence too highly to work 16 hours a day inside a factory, and they found the new machines difficult to master. Arkwright was forced to hire poor children and orphans—"their small fingers being active"—as spinners and weavers. By 1790, his mills employed as many as 5,000 workers, most of them children.

Hiring children was a standard practice during the Industrial Revolution, a practice justified by Smith's *laissez-faire,* or "what the market will bear," economic philosophy. It was natural, Smith wrote, that employers wished to keep wages as low as possible without actually starving the workers to death. If there was competition for laborers, then wages were high; if there were few jobs, or if the employers agreed

JOSIAH WEDGEWOOD (1730-95)

As industrialization brought a higher standard of living to those people employed in the new mechanized industries and those who traded in the new mass-produced commodities, the middle class found itself able to afford not only the necessities but also the "decencies." For a housewife, the necessities were a soup pot and a frying pan; the decencies, a tea service made by Wedgewood.

The genteel habit of tea drinking had only recently been adopted (the lower classes had traditionally taken beer with their meals), and a Wedgewood tea service was considered the centerpiece of a woman's table. Consistently fine workmanship, mass production, and low prices made Wedgewood's crafts unique among the competition. Quality control was Josiah Wedgewood's principal demand; it was said that he limped (his knee had been

This 1809 lithograph depicts men and women of fashion perusing china and statuary at Josiah Wedgewood's London showroom. Wedgewood was one of the first entrepreneurs to open a store in the city for retail sales while maintaining his factory in the country, thus bypassing the middleman and keeping prices down. (The New York Public Library Picture Collection)

disabled since childhood) through the workshops, smashing any cup, plate, or saucer he considered "not good enough for Josiah Wedgewood."

One of England's first and most successful entrepreneurs, Josiah Wedgewood was a third-generation potter. He was also an amateur scientist who tirelessly experimented with new glazes, kilns, and marketing techniques. Rising from poor apprentice to founder of Etruria, his extensive pottery works in Staffordshire, Wedgewood developed new shapes and colors for pottery, even using a steam-powered machine to mechanically stamp designs. He invited famous artists to create fashionable, classic designs for dishes and vases, and created a craze for "jasper," the unglazed porcelain-like pottery he had invented. Smoke from the Wedgewood pottery kilns choked the surrounding countryside as his workers struggled to fill orders for vases and dishes.

In the past, the English aristocracy had imported its dinnerware from China, but as Josiah Wedgewood's standards of perfection became renowned his pottery became a viable alternative to expensive imports. In 1765, Queen Charlotte, the wife of George III, commissioned a set of china. The elegant cream-colored dishes, named "Queen's ware" in a brilliant marketing ploy, became all the rage. So great was the master's reputation that, in 1773, he was commissioned to design a 965-piece dinner service for Catherine the Great of Russia.

Almost single-handedly, Wedgewood took pottery out of the craft workshops and made it a national industry. Successfully implementing new theories on the division of labor, Wedgewood trained his workers to specialize in a particular task, thus "making," he boasted, "such machines of men as cannot err." He also cofinanced such forward-looking projects as a canal linking Etruria to the financial center of Liverpool, thereby drastically reducing his costs for supplies and shipping. A fervid abolitionist (a person who fought to outlaw slavery and the slave trade), he designed a medallion showing a man kneeling in chains with his shackled hands outstretched, encircled by the words "Am I not a man and a brother?" It became the trademark of the abolitionist movement.

Wedgewood's children continued his commercial and experimental legacy. His son Tom was one of the first "dabblers" in photography and published the first essay in English on that subject. He was also the friend and benefactor of Samuel Taylor Coleridge, one of the great Romantic poets. Susannah Wedgewood, Tom's younger sister, became the mother of Charles Darwin (the originator of the theory of evolution), while Josiah II ran the pottery works (which are still thriving today). Josiah Wedgewood died at the age of 65, satisfied that he had built, as he said, "a business which has done me no discredit."

among themselves to a set rate for wages, then pay was low. Orphaned or poor children, untrained in any traditional craft and lacking other means of support, were forced by the market to accept the often inhuman conditions of factory life.

Early Factories

One of England's earliest factories was built in 1742 by the Lombe brothers. Housed in a five-story building (huge for those days), and powered by a waterwheel, the factory was greatly admired by Smith and described as a modern wonder by the novelist Daniel Defoe. Its machines toiled round the clock, wrote Defoe, producing "73,726 Yards of Silk-thread every time the Water-Wheel goes round, which is three times in one minute." The factory was staffed by children working 14-hour to 16-hour shifts, who "cooked their meals on the grimly black boilers, and were boarded in shifts in barracks where, it was said, the beds were always warm."

As the number of factories increased, manufacturing cities were inundated with migrant workers. The Enclosure Act had pushed poor farmers and squatters from their farms, and these new laborers would do whatever work was available for whatever wages the factory owners advertised, and in so doing they drove down the standard of living for all wage laborers. There was competition for housing as well as jobs, and as people crowded into the poorer sections of town, the slums swarmed with thieves, drunkards, prostitutes, and the vices born of poverty and want. Some people turned to new religious sects for comfort, becoming Methodists, Quakers, or Unitarians. Others looked to the readily available gin for comfort.

Not everyone, however, was aware of the miseries of factory towns. Many saw the new manufacturing cities of London, Birmingham, Manchester, Leeds, and Liverpool as hubs of activity and productivity and as fine examples of England's growing economy. When William Hutton visited Birmingham in 1741, he found there a "vivacity" that he had never seen before. "I had been among dreamers," he wrote, "but now I saw men awake."

Within the short span of Adam Smith's life, England transformed itself through new progressive modes of doing business and producing goods. From then on, the pursuit of wealth and progress would absorb the country Smith had tagged "a nation of shopkeepers."

CHAPTER ONE NOTES

p. 1   "The prescription for the spectacles . . ." Robert L. Heilbroner, *The Worldly Philosophers* (New York: Simon & Schuster, 1986), p. 41.

p. 3   "the world the image . . ." Heilbroner, p. 41.

p. 5   "machines for turning grass . . ." Robert Blakewell quoted in Asa Briggs, *A Social History of England* (New York: Viking Press, 1983), p. 172.

p. 5   "as one farm the lands . . ." William Cobbett quoted in Arnold Toynbee, *The Industrial Revolution in Britain* (Gloucester, Mass.: Peter Smith, 1980), p. 3.

p. 6   "It was a frequent complaint . . ." W. T. Selley, *England in the Eighteenth Century* (London: Adam & Charles Black, 1949), p. 199.

p. 6   "With the greater part of rich people . . ." Adam Smith quoted in Heilbroner, p. 73.

p. 6   "Just look at the possessions . . ." Adam Smith quoted in D. D. Raphael, *Adam Smith* (New York: Oxford University Press, 1985), p. 48.

p. 7   "It is not from the benevolence of the butcher . . ." Adam Smith quoted in Heilbroner, p. 55.

p. 7   "I have seen a small manufactory . . ." Adam Smith quoted in Heilbroner, p. 61–62.

p. 8   "For to what purpose is all the toil . . ." Adam Smith quoted in Heilbroner, p. 74.

p. 8   "governments are spendthrift . . ." Adam Smith quoted in Heilbroner, p. 69.

p. 9   "even old barns, cart-houses and outbuildings . . ." quoted in Selley, p. 198.

p. 11   "not good enough for Josiah Wedgewood" Anthony Burton, *Josiah Wedgewood* (New York: Stein and Day, 1976), p. 192.

p. 11   "making such machines of men . . ." Josiah Wedgewood quoted in Burton, p. 31.

p. 12   "a business which has done me . . ." Josiah Wedgewood quoted in Burton, p. 217.

p. 12   "73,726 Yards of Silk-thread . . ." Daniel Defoe quoted in Heilbroner, p. 44.

p. 12   "cooked their meals . . ." Heilbroner, p. 44.

p. 13   "I had been among dreamers . . ." William Hutton quoted in Briggs, p. 186.

p. 13   "a nation of shopkeepers" Adam Smith quoted in Heilbroner, p. 52.

THE STEAM AGE

Industry did not begin during the Industrial Revolution. Long before Richard Arkwright built his cotton mill, such goods as cloth, stockings, blown glass, printed books, beer, and wooden ships were manufactured in England's workshops, cottages, and shipyards by skilled and often well-paid laborers. (Stocking knitters were sometimes so prosperous that they decorated their hatbands with £5 notes.) The contrast between early industries and the industries of the Mechanical Age lay in production methods. The Industrial Revolution brought the factory, the factory method, new machines, and new ways of powering the machines. It was also, in the historian Paul Johnson's words, "the age, above all in history, of matchless opportunities for penniless men with powerful brains and imaginations."

THE NEW ENTREPRENEURS

The unlikely herald of this new age was Richard Arkwright. Although he became known as "the father of the factory system," Arkwright was tagged "rough and unpleasing" by his contemporaries. His mind was "as coarse as it was bold and active," his appearance "plain, almost gross." Despite a lack of formal education—it was said he could scarcely read or write—Arkwright was able to look at something and improve upon it.

Innovation, however, was not without its perils. London weavers in the late 17th century rioted and smashed the new looms introduced by French émigrés. In 1733, after John Kay invented the fly shuttle, which needed only one weaver instead of two to tend it, a band of weavers demolished his house and he was forced to flee the country.

Arkwright was as fearless as he was imaginative and hardworking. In 1768, after years of, as he described it, "intense and painful application," he built a spinning machine in which wooden rollers turning at different speeds twisted carded cotton onto spindles. Investors were impressed by the result: firm, coarse cotton thread stronger than any made before. For the first time in British history, weavers could use domestically produced yarns to thread their looms. England could now undersell the cloth of every other nation.

Arkwright and his partners hired clockmakers—the only people who understood gears in that machineless age—to install these spinning machines in his first factory in Nottingham. The machines were driven by horsepower. A large crank linking all the machines ran from the factory outside to the yard, where it was turned by a harnessed team of sturdy horses.

Horsepower proving too expensive, Arkwright built a larger factory on a river in Derbyshire and powered his machines by waterwheel. (The force of the water's current turned a large paddle wheel that was connected to the machinery's crank.) He then set about inventing machines for carding, drawing, and roving—the operations that transform raw cotton into thread. For the first time, these various processes were combined in one factory operation.

Fledgling entrepreneurs, noting Arkwright's success, rushed to buy his machines and set up factories of their own. Related ventures, such as the printing of patterns on woven cloth, became lucrative as well. Robert Peel, a cottage weaver, revolutionized the way in which calico was printed by using a new technique that he had developed at his kitchen table. Within the decade, Peel was not only printing calico but manufacturing his own cloth and employing 15,000 workers.

So fluid was British society in the early 19th century that money quite literally "made the man." Peel's great wealth and industrial might led, as Arkwright's did, to a knighthood. His son and namesake went to Harrow and Oxford with the sons of the aristocracy (including the aspiring poet Lord Byron). The young Robert Peel collected art, married the great beauty of the day, became involved in politics, and was eventually elected prime minster of England.

Arkwright himself became a magistrate (a local judge). He continued his practice of working 16-hour days, driving his carriage at top speed between the numerous mills he owned, supervising operations. When his spinning mill at Chorley (one of the first steam-powered mills in England) was burned to the ground by a mob of angry hand-spinners, he began rebuilding before the ashes had cooled. He bought a castle with the returns of giving the "unprofitable poor" (his words) gainful employment. Wherever an Arkwright factory was built, other factories sprang up and a manufacturing center came into being. In the last years of his life, Arkwright was knighted by George III for his "services to His Majesty's subjects in general." He left his heirs £500,000 and an industrial empire.

THE NEW METHODS

Cotton clothing had become so inexpensive it had replaced the woolens traditionally worn by working people. Calicos and Indian-cotton prints became popular summer wear for the gentry. Cottons were also easier to wash than wool or linen, and this contributed to the improved sanitary conditions of the 19th century.

The burgeoning textile industry instantly affected the national economy. In 1700, Britain had imported a million pounds of raw cotton; by 1789, imports reached more than 32 million pounds. Textiles made up more than 50 percent of British exports in 1750, and more than 60 percent by 1800. Raw cotton was plentifully available, grown and picked by slaves on the plantations in South America and the Caribbean.

Because of its adaptability to machine production, cotton paved the way for new manufacturing methods, but the iron and coal industries were soon modernized as well. In 1712 Thomas Newcomen, an iron-monger (hardware salesman) and occasional preacher, invented an engine that was used to pump water from coal mines, allowing miners to dig deeper into the earth to tap more profitable veins of coal.

Newcomen began his experiments with the same kind of cylinder and piston-powered pump that the ancient Romans had used to lift water from their mines. He added a brewer's (beer maker's) copper kettle to store water and a furnace to heat the water, and then installed a water jet inside the piston cylinder to condense the steam. When the water boiled, and the steam condensed, it then forced the piston to move within the cylinder, creating a vacuum. The weight of the atmosphere above the piston then pushed the piston down. The force of this up-and-down movement was harnessed to a "walking beam," a huge horizontal beam of wood that balanced like a seesaw and was connected at one end to the piston of the pump. The Roman-style piston pump had been worked by shifts of sweating men and horses; now, powered by the Newcomen engine, the pump could accomplish in 48 hours what 50 men and 20 horses laboring 24 hours a day had accomplished in a week. Some historians have even argued that the invention of steam power signaled such a drastic change in humanity's use of natural resources that the Industrial Revolution should really be called the Steam Age, as previous epochs were known as the Bronze Age or the Stone Age.

The profitability of Newcomen's engine was immediately evident as flooded mines reopened and more miners were employed to work the pits. For the first time in history, humankind had a working mechanical engine. By 1769, there were 120 Newcomen engines in use at coal mines. A French engineer who visited a mine to see one of the engines at work compared it to the human body.

Heat is the cause of [the engine's] motion, as circulation takes place in its different tubes like that of blood in the veins; it has valves that open and close at the proper moment; it feeds itself, it rejects what it has used at regular intervals, it draws from its own work everything that it required for its support.

In 1764, a young mathematical-instrument maker named James Watt looked at Newcomen's invention and saw an expensive, inefficient coal-guzzler. He agreed with those who complained that "it took an iron mine to build a Newcomen engine and a coal mine to keep one going." Watt was attending a lecture on steam heat at the University of Glasgow when it occurred to him that the waste of heat between piston strokes was the source of the Newcomen engine's inefficiency. Building model after model in the college basement, he sought to remedy

THE MECHANICAL AGE

This early diagram of a Newcomen engine shows the domed furnace where the water was heated; above it, the piston that, through the force of steam power, moved the huge walking beam; and, on the right, the working crank that was connected to either a pump or factory machinery. (From J. T. Desaguliers, *A Course in Experimental Philosophy*, vol. 2, 1744)

this problem. Finally, in the spring of 1765, an idea struck him while he was out walking. "I had gone as far as the herd's house," he said, "when the idea came into my mind that as steam was an elastic body it would rush into a vacuum and if a connection were made between the cylinder and an exhausting vessel, it might there be condensed without cooling the cylinder."

Four years later, after various frustrating disappointments, Watt hit upon a working improvement. Watt connected a separate chamber for

HENRY BESSEMER (1813-98)

By the time Henry Bessemer turned his formidable skills to steel making, he already was a wealthy inventor. Energetic and insatiably curious, Bessemer was the son of a French émigré who had fled the French Revolution. His father encouraged the boy's engineering bent and allowed him to stay home from school so that he could rig strange experiments in his workshop, "making models," as Bessemer later wrote, "of the too-numerous schemes which the vivid imagination of youth suggested." When he was 17, Bessemer set off to London with an idea for mass-producing wax casts for sculptors; no one was interested. He invented dies for stamping ornamental scrollwork on Bibles; no one was interested. In 1832, he came up with a "gold dust" machine that ground the pigment for the gold paint used to decorate china. Unlikely as it may seem, this was the contraption that made him a fortune.

Bessemer married and bought a house in London, where he built a spacious, perfectly equipped workshop complete with a large furnace, a foundry for his experiments with iron. Soon he had modified his furnace with a perforated bottom through which air could be blown. This furnace—which became known as the Bessemer converter—was mounted on supports, called trunnions,

steam condensation to the cylinder, and contained both chamber and cylinder in a "steam jacket" to keep its walls hot. Thanks to these minor but fundamental alterations, the engine now consumed a fourth of the fuel it had formerly required.

In 1769, Watt further improved his engine, adding an air pump to the condenser and introducing, as he wrote, "the expansive force of steam to press on the pistons." He also invented safety gauges for steam pressure and temperature, and in 1787 replaced the wooden working beam—most often a huge fir tree 2 feet wide, 5 feet thick and 10 feet long—with a hardier, more cost-efficient beam cast from iron.

nions, that allowed it to be tilted forward and backward. First, Bessemer started the blast of air and poured half a ton of molten pig iron into the converter. Oxygen in the air kept the mass burning, so no additional fuel was needed. When the volcano-like mass stopped burning, Bessemer saw that he had produced in a matter of minutes as much malleable iron as one puddler could have made in hours of work. This malleable iron was, in fact, steel. Traditionally, steel had been painstakingly rolled or hammered from iron that had been packed with powdered charcoal and heated "to a cherry-red heat" for 10 days. Thanks to Bessemer's converter, what had been available only in small quantities at high prices could now be mass-produced. The Bessemer converter could make 20 tons of steel in 20 minutes.

In 1855, Bessemer patented his process of manufacturing malleable iron and steel "without fuel" and built the Sheffield Steel Works. He reaped royalties of up to £5 million from his patents alone. By the year 1868, Britain was producing 110,000 tons of steel. Steel rails were laid for the British railways in 1857, and the first Bessemer steel beams were used to construct the earliest skyscraper—Chicago's Home Insurance Building—in 1884. Bessemer, knighted for his efforts in 1879, never stopped experimenting; his motto, he explained, was "Onward ever!" When he died, he was the holder of 120 patents.

Watt's engine was improved with the financial help of his partner, Matthew Boulton, a Birmingham manufacturer who "badgered" Watt into developing a rotative engine that used a crank and fly-wheel. The flywheel acted as a reservoir of energy, releasing energy as the crank passed through dead center and storing energy during the rest of the stroke. Watt attached his steam engine to a crank as a way of turning gears, and soon textile mills, iron furnaces, flour mills, saw mills, and many other industries were steam-powered.

The business of Boulton & Watt built a new foundry in 1796 and sold its revolutionary engines to everyone from potters to beer makers to printers. As Boulton put it, "I sell what all the world desires to have—power!" The use of steam power was so common by 1850 that definite standards had to be set for determining the capacity of these engines. Since horses had been used for so many centuries to turn cranks, horsepower seemed the natural unit of measure. Watt standardized the figure of 33,000 foot-pounds per minute as one *horsepower.* One foot-pound is defined as the amount of power needed to lift one pound one foot. (The unit of measure of an electrical power unit was later named the *watt* in honor of this tireless inventor.)

IRON

The most crucial problem facing the manufacturers who depended upon steam power was the difficulty in replacing the engines' hand-hammered iron parts. Iron was still produced by laborious old-fashioned techniques and was difficult to purchase in large quantities. The historian Christopher Hill called iron "the chief bottleneck holding back the advance of industry" at this time.

Iron had been manufactured in England since the Middle Ages, when it was found that burning wood in contact with certain ores created a metallic substance called pig iron. Medieval metalworkers discovered that if they hammered and reheated this substance it would become softer and free of impurities. The problem was that iron manufacture required a huge amount of firewood, something in short supply in Britain; by the 18th century there were already severe shortages of wood. This made iron both expensive and hard to come by, a situation that was made worse when shipbuilders for the Royal Navy agitated for laws to protect England's disappearing forests. Finally, in an effort to correct the problem, the government offered rewards to any inventor who could find a way of manufacturing iron using a fuel other than wood.

Beginning in 1709, Abraham Darby began the long process of perfecting a way of producing iron using coke (low-grade coal baked in ovens) to supplement charcoal (burned wood). After many years of experimentation, he became so successful at producing fine-quality iron at low prices that he was soon producing the parts necessary for steam engines in large quantities. The efficient standardization of both parts and tools would put England in the forefront of every other mechanized nation.

In 1784 Henry Cort, a Plymouth ironmaster, developed the process of "puddling" iron. In this efficient and economical way of removing iron's impurities, the flame and gases in Cort's innovative furnace swirled over a bed of sand, the resting place for molten pig iron. The fact that the metal did not come in contact with the fuel and so did not absorb as many of its impurities meant that the pig iron was that much easier to purify. Wrought iron could now be obtained directly from pig iron by using coke rather than charcoal.

Cort's puddling and rolling process perfectly complemented Darby's coke pig iron process. Soon, Britain was exporting huge quantities of wrought iron, as well as the processes themselves.

After the invention of the puddling process, pig iron production increased fourfold between 1740 and 1788, and quadrupled again during the next 20 years. These increases affected many other industries, including agriculture, where iron plows and tools helped make farm labor more efficient.

It was the millionaire ironmaster John Wilkinson, working with Darby's grandson, also named Abraham Darby (1750–91), who cast the arched ribs of the world's first iron bridge. Wilkinson had ordered one of the first Watt engines in 1775 and pioneered the application of steam power to the "rolling" process in iron manufacturing. In 1787, he launched the first iron vessel, a barge 70 feet long and constructed of riveted iron plates. Wilkinson was also successful at marketing his product. He became a household name as he toured the countryside in his iron boat, accompanied, as always, by his famous iron coffin. He promised to return as a ghost to inspect his blast furnaces, and after his death a candlelit vigil outside his foundry was held by people hoping to spot his apparition.

The inventions of these ingenious men radically altered British industry, transforming the textile, iron, and coal industries into prosperous enterprises with huge markets overseas. In 1866, a magazine reporter even went so far as to exclaim:

> Engineering has done more than war and diplomacy; it has done more than the Church and the Universities; it has done more than abstract philosophy and literature. It has done . . . more than our laws have done . . . to change society.

CHAPTER TWO NOTES

p. 15   "the age, above all in history . . ." Paul Johnson, *The Birth of the Modern* (New York: HarperCollins, 1991), p. 188.

p. 15   "rough and unpleasing" and "as coarse as it was bold . . ." Leonard M. Fanning, *The Fathers of Industries* (Philadelphia: Lippincott, 1962), p. 30.

p. 16   "intense and painful application" Richard Arkwright quoted in E. Royston Pike, *"Hard Times": Human Documents of the Industrial Revolution* (New York: Frederick A. Praeger, 1966), p. 31.

p. 17   "unprofitable poor" and "services to His Majesty's . . ." Fanning, p. 36.

p. 18   "Heat is the cause of . . ." Richard Shelton Kirby et al., *Engineering in History* (New York: Dover, 1990), p. 165.

p. 18   "it took an iron mine to build . . ." Kirby, p. 166.

p. 19   "I had gone as far as the herd's house . . ." James Watt quoted in Fanning, p. 21.

p. 20   "making models of the too-numerous schemes . . ." Henry Bessemer quoted in Fanning, p. 138.

p. 20   "the expansive force of steam . . ." James Watt quoted in Kirby, p. 167.

p. 21   "to a cherry-red heat" Kirby, p. 293.

pp. 21–22   "I sell what all the world . . ." Matthew Boulton quoted in Fanning, p. 24.

p. 22   "the chief bottleneck . . ." Christopher Hill, *Reformation to Industrial Revolution* (New York: Penguin, 1969) p. 240.

p. 23   "Engineering has done more . . ." quoted in Briggs, p. 190.

"BLACK TREASURES"

In 1851, a 24-ton boulder of coal was placed at the entrance of the Exhibition of Works of Industry, a forerunner of the World's Fair, as "a symbol of the inestimable value of this grimy mineral to commercial enterprise." It was precisely because manufacturers needed more and more coal to fuel their various enterprises that innumerable inventions were developed, roads improved, canals dug, and railroads built. As early as 1738, an assembly of glassmakers, beer brewers, whiskey distillers, sugar bakers, soap boilers, blacksmiths, cloth dyers, brick makers, lime burners, ironworkers, and calico printers appeared before Parliament to complain about the high cost of coal. This occurrence shows two things about the coal industry: the extent to which coal was used to fuel manufacturing, and the joint concern of all industries to lower its cost.

THE HISTORY OF COAL MINING

The history of coal mining in Britain goes back to the 16th century, when coal dug from shallow holes in the ground supplemented firewood as a fuel. By 1690, surface mines were yielding as much as 3 million tons of coal a year—more than twice what France was producing. Most British mines were owned by an individual, usually an aristocrat, who employed a scant dozen or so workers. Until the 19th century, these colliers were bound to their owners for life, and if the mine were sold, they were deeded over like property to the purchaser. If a miner tried to leave the mine or its surrounding region, he would be hunted down and brought back. Sometimes, fines of up to £100—a fortune for someone making as little as 8 pence a week—would be levied on the escapee.

The actual methods for mining coal did not change very much until the 1850s. "Longwall" mining, in which a seam of coal was removed without cutting away any of the sand or clay that might surround it, was the most common technique. "The working space, running the length of the face, was supported by wooden props," the mining historian John Temple explains, "and, as the work advanced further into the seam, the props were moved up and the empty space behind them filled with the waste, the 'goaf' or 'gob.'" Hewers used picks to hack out the seam, and because the passages were often very narrow, the hewer was forced to lie on his back or side and pick upward—a process that required great skill. One visitor marveled at the sight of a hewer

nearly naked, lying upon his back, elevating his small sharp pickaxe a little above his nose, and picking into the coal-seam with might and main; another . . . is cutting a small channel in the seam, and preparing to drive in wedges. By one or other kind of application the coal is broken down; but if too hardly embedded, gunpowder is employed, and the mineral blasted; the dull, muffled roof-shaking boom that follows each blast startling the ear of the novice, who commonly concludes that the whole mine has exploded and that his last minute is at hand. . . .

Coal was carried in wicker baskets—called "tubs" or "corves"—that could hold 500 pounds of coal each and were pushed along the seams to the shaft by women and children. In some mines, described by Friedrich Engels in *The Condition of the Working Class in England,* "women and children . . . crawl[ed] on their hands and knees fastened to the tub by a harness and chain which [was] generally passed between their legs . . . [others pushed] the tub with . . . head and hands." (He

This 1842 lithograph of a bare-breasted woman miner wearing a belt-and-chain was called "the picture that shocked England." She is pulling a tub of coal through a narrow tunnel—a job that fell to ponies after women were barred from the mines. (From *The Royal Commission Report on the Employment of Women in the Mines,* 1842)

noted with horror the many bald patches and sores on women miners' heads.) When wheeled wooden cars (called "trams") that ran on cast-iron rails (called "plates") and could be pulled by ponies were first introduced, one miner was so grateful he wrote a celebratory poem:

God bless the man in peace and plenty
That first invented metal plates;
Draw out his years to five times twenty,
Then slide him through the heavenly gates.

Traditionally, miners got the coal out of the pit by carrying it up ladders in wicker corves strapped on their backs. In Scottish mines, little girls 6 to 11 years old usually did this job. A girl's basket was loaded with coal and the straps were placed over her forehead. The child, bent forward to bear the weight, would then climb the series of ladders ascending to the pit's mouth; a witness to this process observed that "the height ascended, and the distance along the roads added together, exceed the height of St. Paul's Cathedral" (London's tallest building). Each journey was called a "rake" and children were expected to make 10 to 14 rakes a day.

In the late 17th century, miners used a windlass, a cranked contraption for hoisting that was fixed over the mine shaft to lift the corves.

WOMEN COAL MINERS
IN BRITAIN

"When the 18-year-old Victoria became Queen in 1837," wrote the social historian Richard Pike, "there were several thousands of her sex (many of them younger than she was) working in coal mines in Britain." Wives had traditionally helped their collier husbands, but as mining became a more complicated and dangerous endeavor, and as the mines burrowed deeper into the earth's crust, women were generally hired to "work in places where no man, or even lad could be got to labour in." A foreman told a parliamentary committee that women would, without complaint, "work in bad roads, up to their knees in water, [and] in a posture nearly double."

Most often, female colliers pushed or pulled tubs of coal from the shafts to the pithead, where the coal was sorted and loaded for transport. These women were called "drawers," and Betty Harris, a 37-year-old mother of two, was interviewed by a parliamentary investigator in 1842. "I . . . work from six-o'clock in the morning to six at night," she told him.

> I have a belt round my waist, and a chain passing between my legs, and I go on my hands and feet. The road is very steep . . . it is very hard work for a woman. The pit is very wet where I work, and then water comes over our clog-tops always . . . I have drawn till I have had the skin off me; the belt and chain is worse when we are in the family way. My feller has beaten me many a time for not being ready.

The women who worked as "bearers" had an even harder time of it. A bearer's day began before dawn. Her husband and older

Windlasses were traditionally cranked by women, but eventually became horse-powered so that heavier loads could be lifted. When the horse circled the shaft, a rope was wound or unwound on a drum, raising or lowering men and materials. Because horses were not strong sons would generally go to work around eleven o'clock at night, hewing coal from the wall of the mine. At 1:00 A.M., the woman and her older daughters would leave the youngest children with an elderly neighbor (mixing a little whiskey in the child's milk to keep it quiet) and descend into the pit with their baskets. These bearers loaded the hewed coal into baskets, and with the mother leading, holding a lighted candle in her mouth, the women would painfully begin to climb to the mouth of the pit. Each woman took on a load of 170 pounds, pushing and pulling it 150 yards up the slope of the coal tunnel, up some steep stairs, and out of the pit to where the coal was dumped. A woman would make this trip 24 times during a day's work. The weight of the coals brought to the pit top in a day's work by an average woman was 4,080 pounds. Her wage was 8 pennies a day.

Such findings shocked the public—especially after it was revealed that some women actually picked the coal with the men while dressed in men's trousers. A parliamentary report detailing these inhumane working conditions shocked the public, and in 1842 an act was passed forbidding the employment underground of women and children under 10. Horses and mules were brought in to do their jobs.

Unfortunately, this did not necessarily improve the lives of the women and children in miners' families. Many worked because their families needed their wages to live, and without the extra money coming in each week, the women, for the most part illiterate and with no other skills, were forced to become laundresses or prostitutes to ward off financial ruin. However, as one Scottish woman told a mining commissioner: "I wouldna gang down again"—or, in standard English, "I would not go down again."

enough to raise a load of coal to the surface in a single lift, winding had to be done in two or three stages, and this was a very cumbersome process. The problem was not solved until 1784, when James Watt and Matthew Boulton developed a steam winding engine that could raise any load from the bottom to the top of the deepest mine in just one stage. But these steam engines twisted and rocked as their loads were hoisted to the surface, and it was difficult to find a winding rope strong enough to withstand the immense weight and strain of single-stage lifting. Countless accidents led to the introduction of iron guides, which were built up the sides of the shaft to stop the loads from swinging. The corves were replaced by iron cages into which tubs of coal were wheeled before the cage was pulled to the surface by huge wire ropes, some of which cost as much as £500 a length.

Water and Fire

There were two problems that had to be solved before coal mines could become truly profitable. First, there was the problem of flooding in the tunnels. In 1699, Thomas Savery developed a small machine to drain mines, but it was not very efficient. Finally in 1712 Thomas Newcomen developed a pumping engine that could raise 120 gallons of water more than 153 feet in one minute. With the problem of flooding alleviated, it was soon possible to sink mines so deep that it took a miner as much as an hour to descend the ladders into the tunnels.

The second problem was the lack of ventilation in the mines. Chokedamp, a suffocating mixture of nitrogen and carbon dioxide, caused serious health problems for miners, most of whom, according to Friedrich Engels in *The Condition of the Working Class in England*, died of respiratory problems before the age of 50. Even more serious was firedamp, a mixture of air and methane that exploded when it came in contact with a spark or candle flame. Firedamp was the cause of innumerable blasts and cave-ins, and in the 17th and 18th centuries attempts were made to control its explosions by "firing" it periodically, before it had a chance to build up. A "firer" encased in wet cloth had the thankless job of crawling along the tunnel floor carrying a pole topped by a lit candle "with whose flame the [firedamp] meeting, breaketh with violence." Obviously, this method was extremely dangerous. Using candles or lanterns to light the miners' work was dangerous as well.

A terrible explosion in May 1812 at the Felling Pit in Durham left 92 people dead; the cause of the disaster was an oil lamp igniting firedamp. The sight of the massed coffins, and the affecting sermon

This 19th-century lithograph of a Birmingham coal mine shows the high chimneys of the coke furnaces, the waste heaps of worthless rock, and the railroad tracks for transporting coal to market. (The New York Public Library Picture Collection)

preached to the crowds of mourners, brought even the newspaper reporters to tears. A general call for the invention of a "safety lamp" prompted mine owners to offer a reward to the first engineer or scientist who could produce one.

Sir Humphrey Davy, already famous as England's greatest scientist, went down into the Wall End Colliery in Durham to determine for himself just what was needed. He returned to his laboratory with these parting words to the head engineer: "Do not despair, I think we can do something for you." In January 1816, on Davy's behest, the engineer made an announcement to the press: "I think we have subdued the monster." Davy's invention was a small oil lamp with a burning wick encased in a cylinder of wire gauze. The shape of the wire gauze dispersed the light's heat; if the flame changed color, it alerted miners to the presence of firedamp. Davy refused to take out a patent on his invention, forgoing royalties for the sake of the miners' lives. He was, instead, knighted and awarded £2,000.

THE GREAT STRIKE OF 1844

Despite, or perhaps because of, the rapid growth of the coal industry, a mine remained a dangerous workplace. Cave-ins, explosions, and production accidents were frequent. At the New Hartley mine in Northumberland in January 1862, a pumping engine beam weighing more than 40 tons suddenly fell into the shaft, trapping 204 men and boys in the mine. It took six days to pull the beam out, and by that time all the trapped workers were dead, having been suffocated by poisonous gases.

But miners were unable to demand the high wages that might compensate them for their dangerous occupations. It was not until 1824 that Prime Minister Robert Peel made it lawful for workmen to form unions to determine wages, hours, and working conditions, and decades later that these unions became powerful enough to win concessions from the mine owners. In the meantime, the coal mines, in the words of an article in the *Edinburgh Review*, bore "more conspicuous testimony to human energy and perseverance than the pyramids of Egypt."

One consequence of the severe working conditions in coal mines, the historian Christopher Hill believes, was that mining families became the backbone of the radical reform movement, and their propensity to call a general strike to protest what they considered unfair working conditions was notorious. One of the first large strikes, and one which, if unsuccessful, won many sympathizers, occurred in 1844.

The year before, the miners had formed a union that swelled to some 60,000 members in record time. A committee of miners soon came up with a contract, to be presented to the mine owners, demanding a reform of the pay system. Coal may have been sold to the public by weight, but the miners were paid for the number of tubs they packed. If a tub was not totally filled, the miner was paid nothing or even fined for his load, yet if a tub was overfull the miner was not paid anything extra for the overflow. In *The Conditions of the Working Class in England*, Friedrich Engels contended that a miner might work a week and, because of these fines, actually owe the company money. The new contract proposed that miners be paid by the weight of the coal they cut, not by the tub; that the scales be inspected regularly; and that the fine system be abolished. But the owners refused to recognize either the union or the contract, and on March 31, 1844, 40,000 miners put down their picks and all the collieries of Northumberland and Durham came to a standstill. The owners responded by evicting the miners from company housing. Strikers were forced to spend the five-month duration of the strike living in tents on the moors. The miners were not violent—a fact that greatly impressed the

A "blackleg" is seized by a band of strikers as he leaves the mill. Workers who disregarded the trade union's call for a strike and continued to work were sometimes injured or even killed by union members. (From *The Leisure Hour*, 1862)

general public who read of the strike in the newspapers—except toward "blacklegs," miners who ignored the strike and attempted to go to work. Blacklegs were sometimes injured or even killed by angry bands of strikers.

As the months passed, the situation of the strikers grew more and more difficult. They were prosecuted for trespassing. Their credit was cut off at the local shops. Finally, Irish miners, too poor or too uncaring to feel any loyalty to their fellow miners, were shipped in to do the strikers' work and the strike collapsed. It would be many years before working conditions improved or before it was no longer true that, as an interested observer wrote, "the hardest labour in the worst room in the worst-conditioned factory is less hard, less cruel, and less demoralizing than the labour in the best of coal-mines."

A Mining Village

Coal production doubled between 1730 and 1800, between 1800 and 1830, and again between 1830 and 1845, while the number of miners increased from 216,000 in 1851 to 495,000 in 1881. Coal became the fuel of the Industrial Revolution. It fired everything from the kilns in Josiah Wedgewood's pottery workshops to the boilers of countless factories, as well as the engines of the new locomotives. But the people who hewed, carted, hauled, and broke up the coal were too poor to enjoy the goods and services produced by these industries. The colliers' working conditions were among the worst and their pay the lowest in the nation. They were, in politician the Edmund Burke's estimation, "tortured without remission by the suffocating smoke, intense fires and constant drudgery" of their work.

Typically, mining villages were built around the mine shaft. "Sheds, stables, cottages, [were] stuck into the ground like pins into a pin-cushion" around the countless slag heaps (mounds of "spoil" brought up from the mine's tunnels), the windlass, the engine-house, and the tall chimney of the furnace used to roast coal for iron-smelting. Activity was focused around the smelting furnaces. It was here that the railroads brought the cars loaded with raw coal and carted away the purified coal—"black treasures," in the estimation of a German visitor—to markets in Liverpool or Manchester. The north of England became known as "the black country" as the mines and their accompanying smoke and spoil blackened the environment.

Whole families were employed in the mines. Children became "trappers" whose "duty consist[ed] in sitting in a little hole, scooped out for them in the side of the gates behind each door, where they sit with a string in their hands attached to the door, and pull it the moment they hear the corves at hand, and the moment it has passed they let the door fall to. . . ." (Opening and closing the doors guided the ventilating current of air through the tunnels.) As a boy grew older, he might drive the horses pulling the loaded tub or wagons along the main underground passages. Boys and girls could be promoted to the job of "putting," loading the tubs and pushing and dragging them along the passages.

Children came home from 12-hour shifts exhausted, too tired even to eat their dinners, and their parents often washed and put them to bed while they were asleep. Not surprisingly, mining children suffered many physical ailments. Friedrich Engels recorded with surprise the stunted appearance of mining children; he described a 19-year-old boy who had the body of an 11-year-old. Excessive drinking (even children frequented pubs on the weekends), bad diet, and the unhealthy air of the mines caused their puny stature.

Still, the energy and enterprise of a mining community was awe-inspiring. "To wander amongst 183 collieries congregated in two counties," wrote a reporter for the *Cornhill Magazine* in 1862,

to witness the extraordinary mechanisms and erections for the extraction of coal . . . to note the hundreds of tall chimneys, the streaming black barriers of smoke fuming away in the breeze . . . to stand at a pit's mouth and watch the ceaseless arrival of coaly cargoes . . . [and] the rough and begrimed human beings . . . all this affords a source of interest and excitement which cannot be adequately conceived until it is experienced.

CHAPTER THREE NOTES

p. 25   "a symbol of the inestimable value . . ." Briggs, p. 189.

p. 26   "The working space, running the length . . ." John Temple, *Mining: An International History* (New York: Praeger, 1972), p. 38.

p. 26   "nearly naked, laying upon his back . . ." quoted in E. Royston Pike, *Golden Times: Human Documents of the Victorian Age* (New York: Schocken Books, 1972), p. 69.

p. 26   "women and children . . . crawl[ed] on their hands . . ." Friedrich Engels, *The Condition of the Working Class in England*, trans. and ed. W. O. Henderson and W. H. Chaloner (Oxford, England: Basil Blackwell, 1971), p. 279.

p. 27   "God bless the man in peace and plenty . . ." quoted in Temple, p. 40.

p. 27   "the height ascended, and the distance . . ." quoted in Pike, *Hard Times*, p. 170.

p. 28   "When the 18-year-old Victoria . . ." Pike, *Hard Times*, p. 245.

p. 28   "work in places where no man . . ." and "work in bad roads . . ." quoted in Bonnie S. Anderson and Judith P. Zinsser, *A History of Their Own*, vol. 2 (New York: Harper & Row, 1988), p. 288.

p. 28   "I . . . work from six-o'clock . . ." quoted in Pike, *Hard Times*, p. 256–257.

p. 29   "I wouldna gang down again" quoted in Pike, *Hard Times*, p. 268.

p. 30   "with whose flame . . ." quoted in Temple, p. 44.

p. 31   "Do not despair . . ." and "I think we have subdued the monster" quoted in Johnson, p. 542.

p. 32   "more conspicuous testimony . . ." quoted in Pike, *Golden Times*, p. 78.

p. 34   "the hardest labour in the worst room . . ." quoted in Pike, *Hard Times*, p. 152.

p. 34   "tortured without remission . . ." Edmund Burke quoted in Briggs, p. 177.

p. 34   "Sheds, stables, cottages . . ." Pike, *Golden Times*, p. 78.

p. 35   "black treasures" Briggs, p. 191.

p. 35   "duty consist[ed] in sitting . . ." quoted in Temple, p. 49.

p. 35   "To wander amongst 183 collieries . . ." quoted in Pike, *Golden Times*, p. 64.

ROADWAYS, WATERWAYS, AND RAILWAYS

In the early years of the Industrial Revolution, travel by land or by water was expensive, time consuming, and dangerous. Highwaymen and pirates; uncomfortable coaches and slow, unsanitary ships; dirty and bug-infested inns; and roads rutted with potholes were just a few of the reasons for staying at home. In fact, until the 17th century, a person would often live his or her entire life without traveling more than 100 miles from home.

THE TURNPIKE SYSTEM

In the winter of 1747, the Reverend John Wesley recorded in his diary: "Our servant came up and said, 'Sir there is no travelling today. Such a quantity of snow has fallen in the night that the roads are quite filled up.'" The clergyman's response was typical, both of the age and of his determined personality. He told the man that even if their horses could not get through, "at least we can walk twenty miles a day."

Wesley's reliance on "shank's mare"—as walking was humorously known—for transportation was typical of the period. The poet William

THOMAS TELFORD (1757–1834)

The historian Paul Johnson has called Thomas Telford "the most remarkable man of all, in an age of great men." No other man, singlehandedly, "changed so completely the face of an entire region."

Born into a family of shepherds in an isolated valley in Scotland and apprenticed to a stonemason, the young Telford developed an unusually strong passion for reading and writing poetry. He moved to Edinburgh, where he met William Pulteney, known as "the richest commoner in Britain," who took Telford to Shrewsbury to restore the castle and to be surveyor of public works. Telford built the local jail and various churches before designing and building the Ellesmere Canal, one of the first canals to use the principles of modern engineering while retaining traditional methods. The mortar used to seal the canal's iron plates contained bull's blood "for extra strength." The joints were reinforced with flannel soaked in syrup and boiled for hours.

It was Telford's success as a canal builder that led the British government to select him for what it considered the most important project in the kingdom, transforming the London-Holyhead road. With government funds of £750,000—an extraordinary sum—Telford set about making a straight and speedy road so that "horses may easily and rapidly trot over the whole road, ascending or descending, with a loaded coach," as he put it, at the unprecedented speed of eight miles an hour. A new spirit of organization was combined with what Johnson has called an almost medieval attention to detail, and it took 15 years to complete what was unquestionably the world's fastest road.

Telford wanted to put locomotives on his ideal road system. He believed that "running on rails should be confined to bulk goods and should essentially serve as feeders and outlets to the canal system, a slow but cheap and efficient method of heavy transport." He considered railway lines inefficient; only the company that owned the track could operate the vehicles on it, and the tracks themselves were expensive. Rival companies would build different tracks to compete—more waste, in Telford's eyes. He wanted to reduce the weight of locomotives and to run them on his roads. But the mining and industrial companies were heavily invested in the fixed-track system, and Telford's theories were ignored.

Despite such minor setbacks, Telford's productivity was astounding. All in all, he built more than 1,000 miles of road, nearly 1,200 bridges, as well as harbors, docks, and other structures. All his projects were notable for their beauty as well as their durability. The poet Robert Southey described a Telford bridge as "a spider's web in the air . . . it is the finest thing that ever was made by God or man!"

A 19th-century lithograph of Thomas Telford's Menai Bridge, displaying the graceful lines of its design and its extraordinary suspension system. Note the ship sailing beneath its 100-foot-high arch. (The New York Public Library Picture Collection)

Wordsworth thought nothing of walking 15 miles just to borrow a book, then turning around and walking home again.

Terrible road conditions made the going hard in bad weather. Highways were little more than muddy ditches following the tracks of the old Roman roads (Britain had been under Rome's rule from 43 to 436 A.D.), or winding cow paths that twisted and turned to skirt every large rock or stream. Daniel Defoe witnessed an old lady "drawn to church in her coach with six oxen . . . [not] in frolic or humour, but mere necessity, the way being so stiff and deep [with mud], that no horses could go through it." Little wonder that coaches, the mainstay of travel, jolted and bumped their passengers unmercifully, and sometimes even rolled over. An 18th century traveler described coaches "infernal . . . to be avoided by travellers as they would the Devil."

Such primitive conditions meant that raw materials, products, and passengers could not be moved from field, city, or factory in a dependable or economical way. Consequently, at the turn of the century enterprising merchants, factory owners, and farmers and mine owners began to seek new ways to ship goods and raw materials, realizing that profits depended upon improved modes of transportation.

The Scotsman Thomas Telford was the government's choice for chief engineer. He engineered bridges, canals, harbors, waterways, docks, and roads. He based his roads on Roman models, laying a strong foundation of seven inches of crushed stone on soft soil and then spreading a two-inch layer of gravel. As wagon wheels rolled over this surface it compressed into an impermeable surface. Telford's masterpiece was the 300-mile-long road linking London with Holyhead, Wales. His highway reduced the traveling time between these two cities from 41 to 28 hours.

Telford's fellow Scot John McAdam revolutionized road building. He constructed a surface—called macadam—that was thinner, less expensive, and easier to build than Telford's stone highways. McAdam believed that the subsoil had to be thoroughly drained, reasoning that if the road was kept dry, it would be firm and there would be no need for Telford's deep foundations. The gravel he used was ground very fine, and as wagon wheels and horse hooves passed over it, it became firmly packed and essentially waterproof. This meant there were fewer potholes or ruts to slow traffic. Working with his three sons, McAdam had supervised the building of 2,000 miles of road by 1823. These hard-surfaced "macadamized" roads were the envy of Europe.

Road improvements drastically affected traveling times: it took nearly two weeks to travel from London to Edinburgh in 1745, two and a half days in 1796, and around 36 hours by coach or steamship in 1830. The average citizen began to travel more often—and with less inconvenience as inns became more numerous and more comfortable. In 1784, special mail coaches began "dash[ing] up and down to London," wrote the historian R. J. White, " . . . a flying symbol of this dashing, scurrying, highly populous society."

Heavy goods, however, still moved at the unhurried pace of mules and packhorses. Mule trains were a common sight during these years, winding their slow way to London, the principal market. The rates for heavy cargo, such as coal, could be 20 times higher than those for a lighter load, such as wool, and it was common practice for a merchant to raise the price of heavy cargoes after a heavy rainfall. Bad road conditions made ore even more expensive to transport. Clearly, if England was to transform itself from an agricultural and mercantile society into an industrial society, alternatives to mules and horsepower would have to be found.

WATERWAYS

In *The Wealth of Nations*, Adam Smith had recommended that England's canal system be expanded. He believed that goods could be transported over water in spacious flat-bottomed boats at a fourth of the cost of road travel. He also believed that canals would "put the remote parts of the country more nearly upon a level with those in the neighborhood of the town" and thus expand the markets for merchandise and services.

Josiah Wedgewood agreed with Smith, and he began to actively promote canal building. Forced to use packhorses to bring in flint and clay, his raw materials, and to carry out packing cases of his fragile pottery, Wedgewood was desperate for a speedier, more economical mode of conveyance. He was one of the first entrepreneurs to catch "canal mania" and to form a canal-building enterprise to help finance new waterways. Wedgewood himself cut the first sod for the Mersey-to-Trent Rivers canal, known as the Grand Trunk, in the summer of

1766; it would be 10 years before it was completed. The Grand Trunk became the main stem of a canal system that carried coal, corn, all sorts of industrial products, and those travelers who wanted to glide "tranquilly onwards through a continuous panorama of cows, cottages and green fields." Forty-two canals were built in the latter half of the 18th century, and by 1800 there were 1,400 miles of navigable waterways.

Francis Egerton, the duke of Bridgewater, was responsible for concentrating industrialists' attention on the efficiency of canals. Bridgewater, traveling in France, had admired the Languedoc Canal. Its locks, aqueducts, and tunnels made transportation by water possible through mountainous country. Bridgewater owned coal mines near Manchester, and he had been looking for a way to transport his bulky, heavy cargoes from his mines across the mountainous Irwell Valley and into the city of Manchester. He approached James Brindley, a self-educated engineer, and offered him three shillings a day to build a canal.

Brindley knew nothing about canals, but he was both industrious and ingenious. He decided to build a canal that would cross the Irwell River on an aqueduct 40 feet above the stream—the first time such a method had been employed in Britain. The canal was painstakingly excavated by navvies (short for "navigators"—the workmen who excavated with shovels and wheelbarrows), and it was made watertight by layering clay and sand successively. Completed in 1761, the canal was only 18 feet wide, four-and-a-half feet deep, and 10 miles long, but it halved the price of Bridgewater's coal at the Manchester markets.

No one knows for certain how much the canal cost, but the duke of Bridgewater's profits from it were enough to fund his next project: a canal that linked Manchester with the flourishing port city of Liverpool. James Brindley extended the duke's canal on a winding route along the valley, still keeping it level, and then let it down, in a series of 10 locks, 82 feet into the tidewater of the Mersey River. The total cost of the Bridgewater Canal has been estimated at £220,000, but it cut by one-half the freight charges between Liverpool and Manchester.

Flat-bottomed canal boats moving along the Grand Trunk could carry as much as 50 tons of goods—the equivalent of 16 wagons. They were pulled along the rivers by a single horse that walked along a towpath. So numerous did the canalboats become that Defoe mourned the many horses that died from "an Excess of Labour in those heavy Ways."

Between the years 1764 and 1772, privately held corporations managed to link all of England's major navigable rivers, and the Reverend John Wesley observed that canals even "improved" the common people by creating many employment opportunities. For instance, as Wedgewood's potteries flourished after the opening of the Grand Trunk, the population in the area of his potteries increased from 7,000 partially employed in 1760 to 21,000 "abundantly employed, prosperous and comfortable" in 1786. Eventually, Britain had a transport network without parallel in Europe. Many historians believe that the newfound unity of the canal corporations led to cooperation in such fields as banking, iron, and the building of the railways.

BRIDGES

Meanwhile, the British government had resolved to further improve the nation's highways by building some spectacular bridges to replace the river ferries. Once again, Thomas Telford was chosen to do the job. His Menai Bridge, which crossed the Menai Straits in Wales, was a "technical marvel." Designed to let the tallest warships pass underneath the bridge, its arches were nearly 53 feet wide and chained with massive irons to towers 153 feet high so as to give a clearance of 100 feet. No one had ever built a suspension bridge of this size. Each of the 16 chains had links eight feet long and took more than three hours to raise into position, "a terrifying operation which Telford supervised himself." The Menai Bridge opened on January 30, 1826, and it survived heavy traffic and bad weather without any major repairs until 1939. It is still in use today.

The first iron bridge in history was erected by Abraham Darby III and John Wilkinson in 1779 to replace the ferry across the Severn at Coalbrookdale in central England. The Coalbrookdale Bridge had a 100-foot span some 55 feet above the river, cross-braced to support a level roadway 24 feet wide. Each rib was cast in halves 70 feet long and weighing about 38 tons. These were floated from the nearby foundry on barges, raised into place with block and tackle, and joined at the center with cast-iron bolts.

SHIPPING

The modernizing spirit of organization and innovation spread to England's military and merchant navies. Inhabiting an island famous for its Royal Navy, a large proportion of the English population was adept at sailing. Boat traffic was enormous on every river and in every port as fishing boats and independent passenger boats moved fish, people, and goods throughout the country. England had some of the busiest ports in the world, London being the largest. Its harbor was crowded with huge cargo ships called East Indiamen, which could be equipped for voyages of more than six-months' duration to India and China. Newcastle was England's second-largest port and the home of the coal ships; Liverpool was the next largest, with its ships for the trade with America.

PASSENGER SHIPS

The transition from sailing ships to steamships was a long one. In the 1700s, travelers from England to France could wait weeks for the right wind to come up before they could sail, and constant storms made the crossing to Europe or the United States dangerous. All this changed after James Watt invented a rotary steam engine in 1781. Its boiler was too large to be used on board ship, but many engineers in Britain and the United States continued to tinker with the steam engine. In 1807, the steamship, propelled by a huge paddle wheel and looking like a "sawmill mounted on a scow and set on fire," was designed by the American Robert Fulton. This ungainly craft transformed the shipping industry all over the world. The British elaborated on Fulton's original design and launched the first iron steamship across the English Channel in 1820. The iron steamship made the voyage in record time and proved more reliable than sailing ships. Improvements still needed to be made; the steamship's engines demanded so much coal that it was not able to make long journeys, and sailing ships continued to dominate the East Indian and China trade routes.

Most engineers believed that it would be impossible to design a steamship that could carry enough fuel for a long ocean voyage. If the ship was big enough to hold that much coal, they reasoned, it would be too big for the engines to power. Isambard Kingdom Brunel, the unlikely named son of a French émigré, disagreed.

In 1845, he designed the *Great Western*, which was propelled by huge paddle wheels 28 feet in diameter. On its maiden voyage in 1835, it steamed out of Liverpool and made the trip to New York in 15 days—three times faster than a sailing ship—and with 200 tons of coal to spare. Brunel went on to build the *Great Eastern*, the world's largest steamship and the most remarkable venture in iron ship building. Measuring 692 feet from stern to bow, the *Great Eastern* weighed 19,000 tons. It could carry 4,000 passengers and a crew of 400, 8,000 tons of cargo, and 12,000 tons of coal. Brunel modestly called it "the finest ship in the world," but the terribly difficult task of launching such a heavy vessel—its hull alone weighed 12,000 tons—with the primitive hydraulic rams then in use took two months. By then Brunel's health had been broken by the strain, and he died from the complications of a stroke at the age of 56. Even so, the *Great Eastern* was a forerunner of the modern ocean liners.

Henry Bessemer's 1856 invention of an inexpensive method for making steel led to the building of steel steamships that were both lighter and stronger than iron ones and could carry more cargo. In the 1820s, steamships began making trips from England to the United States, Germany, and France, carrying mail, passengers, and freight. For decades the British merchant marine dominated the world's shipping trade. Steamship travel became so routine that ticket prices fell. In 1840, passage from Europe to New York was as low as £5, a little more than two months' wages for the average working man.

RAILWAYS

"Speed—distance—dispatch—are still relative terms," a 19th-century historian wrote, "but their meaning has been totally changed within a few months." The invention that so quickly altered the historian's world was George Stephenson's locomotive. Stephenson, an illiterate engineman at the Killingworth Colliery in northeastern England, invented a working, reliable locomotive in 1814. His was not the first of its kind—locomotives had been used since 1811 to haul coal from the pithead to the ports at less cost—but Stevenson had improved upon the initial design, building 34 different engines before inventing one that could efficiently use steam power for propulsion.

The problem with Stevenson's first locomotive was that its high-pressure engine was not powerful enough; it often required "a good human shove" to get going (Stephenson's sister-in-law often did the pushing while Stephenson and his brother operated the controls). But as Stephenson improved the engine's horsepower, valves, and the traction system of its wheels and rails, his locomotives became more and more fuel efficient.

In 1818, a group of businessmen from the Aukland-Darlington coalfield got together to map out their plan to build a line to transport their coal to Stockton-on-Tees, on the northeastern coast of England. Their first thought was to build a horse-drawn tramway, but Stephenson convinced them to build a railroad that could convey paying passengers as well as coal. The Stockton and Darlington, owned by the Quaker Edward Pease, was the first railway in the world to use a steam-propelled—as opposed to horse-drawn—locomotive. It was 12 miles long, and a huge crowd of 40,000 people watched the *Experiment* pull 21 coal wagons weighing 90 tons over eight miles at eight miles an hour when it opened on September 27, 1825.

Stephenson's next job was as chief engineer of an even more important railway that would link the textile manufacturing city of Manchester with the port city of Liverpool, its supplier for raw cotton. The railway was completed in four years, at which time Stephenson persuaded some local businessmen to sponsor the Rainhill Trials, which would offer a prize of £500 for the best locomotive "which should meet stipulated conditions with regard to weight, speed, and tractive power." The winning model would be the locomotive to run on the line. Stephenson's own son, Robert, competing against three other contenders, was the winner. Drawing a carriage bearing 30 passengers, his *Rocket* reached a speed of 25 miles an hour—the fastest speeds ever achieved. Fanny Kemble, the most famous actress of the day, was one of the first passengers on the Liverpool and Manchester Railway. She described the "sensation of flying" over the rails as "quite delightful and strange beyond description."

Robert Stephenson went into partnership with his father and opened the world's first locomotive works in Newcastle. In 1834, he began working on his greatest project yet, "indeed the greatest construction project . . . since the raising of the pyramids in ancient

This 1829 drawing depicts Robert Stephenson's Rocket *and its coal car. (Note the primitive piston attached to the front wheel.) With Stephenson as engineer, the* Rocket *won the Rainhill Trials with a speed of 25 miles an hour.* (The New York Library Picture Collection)

Egypt"—the building of a London-Birmingham railway. The route was carved out of rock and even went underground in a tunnel excavated by 1,300 navvies using only wheelbarrows, pulleys, and 200 horse-and-wagons. It took more than two years to complete the Kilsby tunnel alone, and the head contractor died from the strain, but the railway opened in September 1838 and proved to be very profitable. By 1850, there were more than 10,000 miles of railroad track crisscrossing Great Britain.

MAIL SERVICE

Mail service was just one of the many enterprises whose efficiency was greatly improved by the railroads. In 1840, the postage stamp was pioneered with the "Penny Black," a 1-pence adhesive stamp. Previously, the recipient had paid the mailman to collect his or her mail—the popular novelist Sir Walter Scott commented that his fan mail cost him £150 a year—effectively keeping poor people from receiving any mail at all. With the invention of the postage stamp, mail delivery increased tremendously. In 1826, London generated as much as 100,000 pieces of mail a day.

The British mail system was soon renowned for its efficiency. In 1821, a letter posted in Manchester by 4 P.M. would be in London the next morning by 10 A.M. The novelist Jane Austen, in *Emma*, paid tribute to the mail service—the "regularity and dispatch of it! If one thinks of all that it has to do, and all that it does so well, it is really astonishing."

DEPARTMENT STORES

With railway lines stretching across England, and merchant ships linking its markets with European ones, fresh fruits and vegetables could be shipped from farms all over the kingdom to the major cities. Such modern conveniences as the department store were also possible. Goods from throughout the nation and Europe were available when the first store of this kind was built in London in 1863 by William Whitely (nicknamed "the Universal Provider"). By the end of the century there were also chains of shops: Jesse Boots, a Northampton druggist, owned 181 local shops, and Thomas Lipton, a grocer, had more than 60 in London alone.

The railroads were a triumph of industrial organization, "an unexampled blending of technological and engineering feats with managerial and financial skill," in the words of the historian R. K. Webb. It took hundreds and hundreds of workmen to build them, extraordinary amounts of money to finance them, and their demand for materials created booms in the related iron and engineering industries. The principal changes in transportation—from wood to steel as a building material, and from sail to steam as a means of propulsion—not only expanded England's markets, but created whole new markets for steel and for coal. "These magnificent enterprises," Webb has written, "had a striking impact on the economy, the ways of life, and the sensibilities of the entire country."

p. 37	"Our servant came up . . ." Henry Thomas and Dana Lee Thomas, *Living Biographies of Religious Leaders* (Garden City, N.Y.: Garden City Books, 1959), p. 248.
p. 38	"the most remarkable man of all . . ." Johnson, p. 179.
p. 38	"changed so completely the face . . ." Johnson, p. 183.
p. 38	"The richest commoner . . ." Johnson, p. 180.
p. 38	"for extra strength" Johnson, p. 179.
p. 38	"horses may easily and rapidly trot . . ." Thomas Telford quoted in Johnson, p. 181.
p. 38	"running on rails should be confined . . ." Johnson, p. 190.
p. 39	"a spider's web in the air . . ." Robert Southey quoted in Johnson, p. 184.
p. 40	"drawn to church in her coach . . ." Daniel Defoe, *A Tour through the Whole Island of Great Britain* (New York: Everyman Editions, 1962), p. 129.
p. 40	"infernal . . . to be avoided by travellers . . ." Arthur Young quoted in Briggs, p. 207.
p. 41	"dash[ing] up and down to London . . ." R. J. White, *Life in Regency England* (New York: Putnam, 1963), p. 10.
p. 41	"put the remote parts . . ." quoted in Heilbroner, p. 65.
p. 42	"tranquilly onwards through a continuous panorama . . ." Briggs, p. 206.
p. 43	"an Excess of Labour . . ." Defoe, p. 530.
p. 43	"abundantly employed . . ." Kirby et al., p. 210.
p. 43	"technical marvel" Johnson, p. 182.
p. 43	"a terrifying operation . . ." Johnson, p. 182.
p. 44	"sawmill mounted on a scow . . ." Johnson, p. 195.
p. 45	"Speed—distance—dispatch . . ." quoted in Kirby et al., p. 277.
p. 46	"a good human shove" Johnson, p. 581.
p. 46	"which should meet stipulated conditions . . ." Kirby et al., p. 278.
p. 46	"sensation of flying . . ." Fanny Kemble quoted in Johnson, p. 191.

p. 46–47   "indeed the greatest construction project . . ." quoted in Richard Tames, *Radicals, Railways and Reform: Britain 1815–51* (London: B. T. Batsford, 1986), p. 45.

p. 48   "regularity . . ." Jane Austen quoted in Johnson, p. 166.

p. 48   "an unexampled blending of technological . . ." R. K. Webb, *Modern England from the 18th Century to the Present* (New York: Dodd, Mead, 1970), p. 269.

p. 48   "These magnificent enterprises . . ." Webb, p. 269.

CHAPTER 5

GENERAL LUDD AND PETERLOO

Sad sixteenth of August! accursed be the day;
When thy field, oh, St. Peter! was crimson'd with gore;
When blue-mantled bullies, in hostile array,
Struck down to the earth the defenseless and poor.
—*Manchester Observer,*
September 18, 1819

The textile industry was one of the first to be mechanized, and cottage weavers were some of the first industrial saboteurs. Before the invention of the spinning jenny and the water frame, spinning had been done at home. Although the work required long hours and the carding and dying processes polluted the cottage's air, the textile worker was an independent and self-sufficient laborer. With the coming of the factory system, unskilled children took over these artisans' jobs. Two steam looms attended by a boy could weave three and a half pieces of cloth in the time a skilled man weaving on a hand-operated loom finished one. Once these artisans realized that their livelihoods were endangered by factory-made goods, they began to fight the new machines with whatever means were at their disposal.

INDUSTRIAL RELATIONS

Generally, the factory owners did not feel responsible for the welfare of their employees. As early as 1776, Adam Smith had deplored the bosses who "with the utmost silence and secrecy" plotted "to sink the wages of labor." Mill owners, in turn, declared that "the only way to make the lower orders temperate and industrious was to lay them under the necessity of labouring all the time they can spare from rest and sleep, in order to procure the common necessities of life." Consequently, wages were kept low and workers lived in flimsy, often filthy housing rented at high rates from the factory owners. These cottages had no running water and often no outhouses. As many as two or three families would crowd into a few rooms, and "the whole of their washings and filth . . . [were] thrown into the front or back street." A laborer's diet was generally potatoes and bread washed down with tea or coffee. Milk, eggs, and bacon were luxuries, and vegetables and fruits were special treats eaten at Christmastime, or not at all.

The new industrial masters became as rich as, or richer than, the aristocracy, but they lacked the gentry's traditional sense of responsibility for the poor. Where the aristocratic lord had traditional obligations, rooted in feudalism, to the tradesmen, farmers, and even the beggars in his area, the relationship between boss and worker was strictly one of cash wages. Conditions within the factory depended a good deal on the character of the manufacturer. The journalist William Cobbett reported that in one cotton mill the workers were actually locked into the mill until dinnertime, and that even in the hottest weather the windows were nailed closed and the water kept under lock and key. In contrast, the Scottish mill owner David Dale provided food, clothes, and the services of a doctor for his workers' children, and Samuel Oldknow disbursed wheat bread, milk porridge, meat, and fruit. But even Oldknow followed the common practice of paying his mill hands with "cheques drawn on his own shop for payment in kind at sight." These "cheques" (also known as "truck") were coupons that could be traded for goods or services at the company store. Because no other store would accept the "cheques," the company store had no competition and thus could charge higher prices for its merchandise.

Many of the workers were accustomed to poverty, and some were making more money than ever before, but on the farms and in the villages where they had previously lived, they had been able to augment their salaries with food from their gardens or by hunting game. Now living in slums, factory workers no longer had gardens to save them from starvation during times of unemployment, sickness, or injury.

The workers attempted to help themselves by organizing trade unions, or "combinations," to assist the unemployed or disabled. They agitated for better working conditions, too, striking, rioting, and petitioning Parliament for wage increases and a shorter workday (14-hour to 18-hour shifts were commonplace). But government was unsympathetic to the petitions of either the workers or the unemployed, and the situation worsened after the French Revolution, when all proposals for reform and all sympathy with the claims and sufferings of the poor were labeled "revolutionary." Although most combinations did nothing more revolutionary than provide the sick and unemployed with benefits, even that was against the mill owners's interests. In 1799, Parliament passed the Combination Act, which punished union membership with three months of imprisonment or two months of hard labor.

THE CORN LAW

The European wars (1792–1803) that followed the French Revolution were particularly hard on British businessmen. England's war with France meant blockaded ports, high taxes, and restricted markets. The Napoleonic War (1803–15) against France and the War of 1812 with the United States further disturbed the cotton, iron, and slave trades. War also meant food shortages. European corn had become a staple of British markets, and as it became scarce domestic corn prices rose dramatically. Wheat cost 43 shillings a quarter (eight bushels) in 1792, the year the French revolutionary wars began, and 126 shillings a quarter in 1812. Although the farmers were reaping huge profits, this situation devastated the poor: a single bushel of wheat cost 14 shillings—twice what the average factory worker made in a week.

While the farmers and their landlords, who had begun to charge exorbitant rents for farmland, made fortunes, the poor were going hungry. Businessmen were forced to raise wages, thus lessening their already bruised profits. A few enterprising merchants hoped to remedy this predicament by importing corn and wheat from abroad and underselling British farmers.

Parliament responded in 1815 by passing the protective Corn Law, which imposed a tariff on foreign imports of grain. The tariff was set high enough to prevent foreign competitors from underselling British corn and wheat. The farmers and landowners, who held most of the parliamentary seats and thus were responsible for setting the tariff, were able to sell their farm products at high prices. But the factory owners, who were not well represented in Parliament, asked: How could foreigners afford to buy our cottons if we refuse their grains?

On the day that Parliament approved the Corn Law, there were riots in London. A mob attempted to storm Westminster, where Parliament met, and ministers were dragged from their carriages. The member of Parliament Sir Frederick Flood was, in his own words, "flung like a mackerel from Billingsgate market. . . . I thought they meant to quarter me." In Sheffield, a mob protested the price of bread by carrying poles topped with blood-stained loaves of bread.

POPULAR UPRISING

The population's discontent was also influenced by the current crisis of the monarchy. The practical but dull King George III had begun talking to trees and was declared incurably insane in 1811, the year his son, the future George IV, was appointed prince regent. The "Regency," as the years 1811 to 1820 became known, were characterized by Prince George's extravagance, drunkenness, vanity, and lack of public spirit. (It was said that the British public respected George III mad far more than George IV sane.) While the regent poured money into his pavilion at Brighton, creating an elaborate, Moorish-Oriental palace to receive his aristocratic guests, hooded bands of "Luddites"— vengeful cottage artisans who had been forced out of business by factories—were attacking machinery and burning down mills.

The radical press championed the workers' cause and called for constitutional freedoms such as those enjoyed by American citizens:

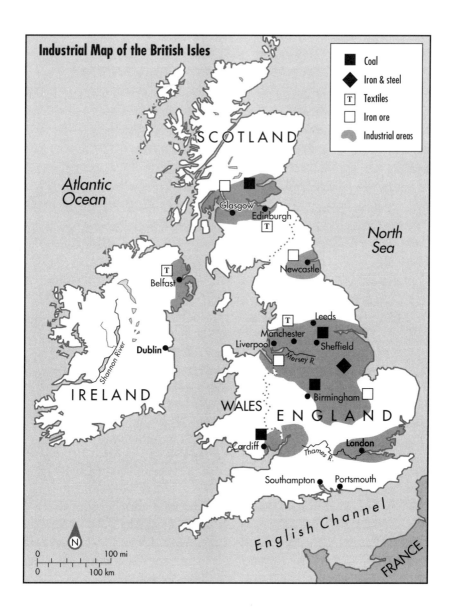

Industrial Map of the British Isles

Coal
Iron & steel
Textiles
Iron ore
Industrial areas

SCOTLAND

Atlantic Ocean

Glasgow
Edinburgh

North Sea

Newcastle

Belfast

Leeds
Manchester
Liverpool
Sheffield

Dublin

Shannon River

IRELAND

WALES

ENGLAND

Birmingham

Cardiff

London

Thames R.

Southampton
Portsmouth

English Channel

FRANCE

0   100 mi
0   100 km

N

freedom of the press, freedom of religion, the rights to bear arms
and to vote. The most popular periodical was William Cobbett's
Political Register, which reached the unprecedented circulation of
50,000 during the fall of 1816. Cobbett's readers were concentrated
in the industrial cities of the north, where the population of workers

THE LUDDITE RIOTS (1811–13)

And by night when all is still,
And the moon is hid behind the hill,
We forward march to do our will
With hatchet, pike, and gun!

Secret handshakes, the password "Free Liberty," and such songs as the one quoted above were the signs of the Luddites, an organized band of stocking weavers. Before the Industrial Revolution, "stockingers," as stocking weavers were called, had operated simple looms by hand. Master stockingers rented their looms from their employers, called hosiers, for a fee, and the work was done in the master stockingers' homes by apprentices and journeymen. Their work was highly skilled and well rewarded.

When Britain declared war on France in 1803, the demand for British stockings dropped, and entrepreneurs seized this moment to set up mechanized stocking frames. Whereas stockingers had knit a seamless stocking, the machines made a large piece of knitted material that was then cut and sewn, often clumsily, into the shape of a stocking. Machine-made stockings were far less expensive than hand-knit ones to make, but they didn't wear well. Still, they sold for less, and the stockingers' wages were, by necessity, cut drastically so that their goods could compete in the open market.

In the winter of 1811, after a bad harvest had sent the price of bread skyrocketing, the stockingers began to petition

was greatest. It was in these cities that confrontations between reformers and authorities became more and more common, and culminated in a massacre.

"Inhabitants of Manchester! The eyes of all England, nay of all Europe, are fixed upon you!" read the announcements of a mass meeting in Manchester, one of the largest factory towns. On August 16, 1819, 30,000 unemployed weavers, farm laborers, war veterans, women, and children made their way to St. Peter's Field. They carried

THE MECHANICAL AGE

government for relief—but no help came. The unemployed and their families were living on oatmeal and potatoes when they banded together and took to the roads, smashing mechanized stocking frames and burning mills. The government responded by making frame breaking an offense punishable by death, but the violence spread, moving northward where the Luddites attacked power looms and burned down mills. There were rumors that the followers of "General Ludd"—after Ned Ludd, a young man who had smashed a labor-saving machine in 1799—numbered in the thousands. In Nottinghamshire during a single week in November, 90 stocking frames were broken. The local people refused to help the authorities apprehend the Luddites, but the mill owners managed to catch and prosecute 13 Luddites in 1813; they were hanged. After soldiers were brought into the area to protect the machines, the attacks dwindled and died.

In 1849, Charlotte Brontë published *Shirley*, a romance set in Yorkshire during the Luddite Riots. Her hero was a mill owner who saw the protection of his machines as a necessity not only for the survival of his business but for the preservation of law and order in the nation. At the same time, the author noted the polluting ugliness of his mill and the sad destitution of the unemployed stockingers. As she described it, the mill yard was a battleground where the "indignant, wronged spirit" of the owners "bears down in zeal and scorn on the famished and furious mass" of workers. These two forces would be defined later as the "two nations" of England, with the Luddite Riots being the first battle of the long "class war" between the rich and the poor.

banners painted with either the workers' symbol—a sharp-bladed pike (a kind of long-handled battle-ax)—or such slogans as "No Corn Laws" and "Equal Representation or Death."

As the workers marched through town accompanied by the sound of fife and drum, many onlookers were convinced that the demonstrators were plotting revolution rather than reform. For days there had been a rumor that "if the country people went with their . . . banners, and music, the soldiers would be brought to them," and notices had appeared around Manchester, warning peace-loving citizens to stay indoors.

The meeting began with Orator Hunt, a leading radical, addressing the crowd on the themes of liberty, suffrage (the right to vote), and governmental corruption. During his speech the Manchester magistrates, pressured by local factory owners, called out the militia. As mounted soldiers pressed forward into the crowd to arrest Hunt, demonstrators linked arms to protect him. Hunt was defiant. He yelled "Stand firm!" and led the crowd in rebellious cheers, when suddenly violence erupted. "I heard the bugle sound," wrote an eyewitness. "I saw the cavalry charge forward sword in hand. . . . The woeful cry of dismay sent forth on all sides, the awful rush of so vast a living mass, the piercing shrieks of the women, the deep moanings and execretions of the men . . . are indescribable." The reporter dove under a carriage as the calvary charged into the crowd, "trampling down and cutting at all who could not get out of their way." Within 10 or 15 minutes, 11 people had been killed and 400 injured—140 from sabre cuts. The weaver Samuel Bamford described the aftermath:

In ten minutes . . . the field was an open and almost deserted space . . . [strewed with] caps, bonnets, hats, shawls, and shoes . . . trampled, torn and bloody. The yeomanry [calvary] had dismounted—some were easing their horses' girths, others . . . wiping their sabres. . . . Several mounds of human beings still remained where they had fallen, crushed down and smothered.

In a bitter pun on the 1814 Battle of Waterloo—a decisive British victory in the Napoleonic War—this conflict was called the Peterloo Massacre.

More than any other single event, Peterloo gave the liberals in British politics the cause that they had been searching for. News of Peterloo spawned more protests in manufacturing towns, particularly after it became clear that the government, rather than enacting reforms, was passing legislation to further restrict the freedom of the press and the freedom of speech.

The Massacre at St. Peter's; *or* Briton's Strike Home! *reads the title of this 1819 drawing. The circulation of such eyewitness accounts in radical newspapers prompted riots and protests all over England.* (The New York Public Library Picture Collection)

Orator Hunt, released on bail, made a triumphant entry into London amid cheering crowds in September 1819. His trial became a *cause célèbre*, but he was ultimately sentenced to two years of imprisonment for disturbing the peace; no soldiers were ever tried for the murders of the protesters. The prince regent, who had publicly supported the Manchester magistrates in the Peterloo controversy, was booed and his carriage pelted with stones and eggs as he passed through the streets of London. Then, on January 29, 1820, George III died. Against the advice of his ministers, the prince planned an elaborate and prohibitively expensive coronation. The nation's mood was so inflammatory that in a letter to a friend, the poet Robert Southey wrote, "At this moment nothing but the Army preserves us from that most dreadful of all calamities, an insurrection of the poor against the rich. . . ."

WILLIAM COBBETT (1763–1835)

Painted while William Cobbett was residing in Newgate Prison, this portrait reveals the luxury of the prison apartments where he received visitors and continued to edit the Political Register. (The New York Public Library Picture Collection)

Many historians believe that it was due to the clear, calming voice of William Cobbett that the riots that followed the Peterloo Massacre did not escalate into a full-fledged civil war. Cobbett, fearing an insurrection on the level of the French Revolution, convinced his readers that riots and machine breaking would only give the government an excuse for further repression. He believed that government reform rather than revolution was the answer. "We want great alteration, modification to suit the times and circumstances," he wrote, "but the great principles [of government] ought to be, and must be the same." Colleague Samuel Bamford believed that the poor were swayed by Cobbett's arguments. "The writing of William Cobbett," explained Bamford, "was read on nearly every cottage hearth in the manufacturing districts. . . . [Its] influence was speedily visible; he directed his readers to the true cause of their sufferings—misgovernment; and to its proper corrective—parliamentary reform."

Historians may disagree on whether William Cobbett was "the noblest English example of the noblest calling of an agitator" or a "noisy Tory Radical," but no one can deny that he was the most influential British journalist of the 19th century. In 1800 he founded the *Political Register*, where, in "plain, broad, downright English," he described the lives of poor people, lectured government officials, and outlined practical ways for British citizens to affect government. Championing abolition, for example, he pushed his readers to boycott the crops exported from slave plantations (cotton, sugar, and coffee) and published recipes for an imitation coffee made of roasted wheat.

In 1810, Cobbett criticized the flogging of soldiers by German mercenaries and was sentenced to two years in Newgate Prison for seditious libel. Some might have been silenced by such treatment, but Cobbett, with the help of some wealthy supporters, paid prison officials £12 a week to live in a comfortable and spacious cell where he continued to edit his paper. In fact, imprisonment only increased Cobbett's fame; he saw friends, wrote against the government, and was, by his own account, visited during those two years by individuals and deputations from 197 different cities and towns throughout Britain and Ireland.

Upon his release, Cobbett continued to comment on the events of the day, and circulation of the *Register* continued to swell. But in 1817, fearing another term of imprisonment for libel, Cobbett went into exile. He farmed for a year on Long Island, in the state of New York, then returned home to undiminished popularity in 1819. Cobbett spoke at political rallies around the country, vilifying what he called "Old Corruption"— the patronage system of government appointments—and in 1832 was elected a member of Parliament. Considered something of a loner by his peers, he followed his conscience in Parliament and was instrumental in the passing of the Great Reform Bill. Reelected in 1835, he was taken ill after a late night of speech making and died at his farm. In its obituary, the London *Times* called him a "self-taught peasant," but Cobbett, as usual, had the last word: he had written his own eulogy. In his own words, Cobbett was a friend of the working people "whom neither the love of gain, nor the fear of loss, could seduce from his duty towards God, towards his country, and towards them. . . ."

p. 52   "with the utmost silence and secrecy . . ." Adam Smith quoted in Hill, pp. 266–267.

p. 52   "the only way to make the lower orders . . ." Hill, p. 273.

p. 52   "the whole of their washings and filth . . ." quoted in Pike, *Hard Times*, p. 49.

p. 52   "cheques drawn on his own shop . . ." Selley, p. 234.

p. 54   "flung like a mackerel . . ." Sir Frederick Flood quoted in Johnson, p. 372.

p. 56   "And by night when all is still . . ." quoted in Erickson, p. 61.

pp. 56–57   "Inhabitants of Manchester! . . ." quoted in Carolly Erickson, *Our Tempestuous Day: A History of Regency England* (New York: William Morrow, 1986), p. 257.

p. 57   "indignant, wronged spirit . . ." Charlotte Brontë, *Shirley* (Oxford: Oxford University Press, 1991), p. 344.

p. 57   "if the country people went . . ." quoted in Erickson, p. 261.

p. 58   "I heard the bugle sound . . ." quoted in Erickson, p. 262.

p. 58   "In ten minutes . . ." Samuel Bamford quoted in E. P. Thompson, *The Making of the English Working Class* (New York: Random House, 1964), p. 687.

p. 59   "At this moment nothing but the Army . . ." Robert Southey quoted in Johnson, p. 432.

p. 60   "We want great alteration . . ." William Cobbett in Green, p. 440.

p. 60   "The writing of William Cobbett . . ." Samuel Bamford quoted in John Stevenson, *Popular Disturbances in England 1700–1832* (London: Longman Group, 1992), p. 275.

p. 60   "the noblest example . . ." G. K. Chesterton quoted in Daniel Green, *Great Cobbett: The Noblest Agitator* (London: Hodder and Stoughton, 1983), p. 6.

p. 61   "plain, broad, downright English" Wiliam Hazlitt quoted in Green, p. 447.

p. 61   "whom neither the love of gain . . ." William Cobbett quoted in Green, p. 465.

REBELS AND ROMANTICS

In the 18th century, European philosophers believed that science would offer them "eternal truths" classifiable in rigid categories and hierarchies. For instance, at the top of the "Divine" hierarchy was God; beneath him in a descending order came angels, humans, animals, insects, and devils. Economics, physics, ethics, and politics could be similarly classified; even the plant world was hierarchical, with mold ranked below flowers and shrubs. Science was challenging this orderly universe, however, and with each scientific discovery and every mechanical invention, humanity learned something new about nature's laws. Consequently, people began to question their old beliefs, and political systems and conventional morality—all the "eternal truths" of the 18th century—came under scrutiny.

This impulse coincided with and was fueled by the French Revolution of 1789, which abolished the French monarchy and the aristocracy. The revolutionary French government in 1793 established a religion of nature worship to replace Catholicism. The ideas of the French philosopher Jean-Jacques Rousseau, who affirmed that a person was born virtuous and was corrupted by society, became as popular in England as in France. The poets, writers, and painters of what became known as the Romantic Movement sought "the child within the man." They embraced Rousseau's statement "I feel therefore I am" and sought their creativity, in the poet William Wordsworth's phrase, in "the spontaneous overflow of powerful feelings."

THE ROMANTIC MOVEMENT

William Wordsworth could be called the "father of the Romantic movement," as Richard Arkwright was labeled the "father of the factory system." In 1797, Wordsworth abandoned city life and moved with his sister, Dorothy, and his friend and fellow poet Samuel Taylor Coleridge to the beautiful Lake District of England. The two poets collected their work in a slim, privately published book called *Lyrical Ballads*.

Wordsworth's poems were written "in the real language of men"—a revolutionary approach at a time when most poetry was written in a self-consciously poetic style and centered on great battles, Greek myths, and aristocratic lovers. Wordsworth's poetry dealt with scenes from real life: descriptions of nature, narratives about war widows, veterans begging on the roads, and unwed mothers who murder their babies. In short, his poems were about people at the mercy of progress and "improvements."

Wordsworth's "naturalistic" poetry and Coleridge's mystical and exotic poems would influence an entire generation of artists. The painters John Constable and J. M. W. Turner and the poets William Blake, Percy Shelley, Lord Byron, and John Keats responded passionately to the *Lyrical Ballads* and its ideas about nature, politics, and art.

Rather than paint the portraits of aristocrats or the "story" pictures illustrating scenes from popular dramas or from history, John Constable decided he would paint, as he said, "the visible world of tree, flower, river, field and sky, exactly as they presented themselves to the senses." His paintings could be called physical representations of Wordsworth's poems. J. M. W. Turner also believed that artists should appreciate the beauty of the sky, trees, and water rather than the creations of humans. In using color rather than line to depict speed, changes of light, and action, he was attempting, he said, to "convey a total sense of truth to nature" and to declare "the independence of color."

Freedom from society's conventions and laws was important to these artists, and many of them deplored what the poet William Blake termed society's "mind-forged manacles." Turner painted a slave ship, Blake equated prostitutes and soldiers with slaves, and Shelley advocated the abolition of the monarchy, deploring

Princes, the dregs of their dull race, who flow
Through public scorn,—mud from a muddy spring,
Rulers who neither see nor feel nor know,
But leechlike to their fainting country cling
Till they drop, blind in blood, without a blow . . .

Most people during this period looked upon nature as the raw material for industry. Few would have considered climbing a mountain, as Wordsworth did, just to see the view. But the Romantics worshiped mountain peaks and precipices, which were "pregnant with religion and poetry." The Romantics particularly regretted the destruction of the English countryside as "dark satanic mills" (in William Blake's words) dirtied the air and streams with sooty wastes. Celebrating the country lifestyles of the peasantry, which were fast disappearing, and the beauty of the natural world, they also advocated "the rights of man"—a phrase from Thomas Paine's popular pamphlet and a political idea then irrevocably altering the United States and France. Some of these artists created their own strange political systems. William Blake became a mystic, the prophetic poet of a political system based on excess and angels and visions. "I have very little of Mr. Blake's company," remarked his wife. "He is always in Paradise."

One of the most talented women of this period was totally unknown except among her small circle of friends. She was a woman who, in the historian Paul Johnson's estimation, might have been a greater poet than her brother if she had had the education and encouragement. She was Dorothy Wordsworth, the sister of William, and from her diaries came the inspiration for many of his poems. Brother and sister lived together, and he read her journal regularly. Its entries were so finely and minutely observed that Wordsworth said simply: "She gave me eyes, she gave me ears." Published in this century, the journal attests to Dorothy's poetic sensibility, but she never completed any

GEORGE GORDON, LORD BYRON (1788–1824)

By'rn, By'rn, By'rn—wherever a person went in polite society, he or she was sure to hear the murmur of his name. George Gordon, Lord Byron, was the most popular poet of his day and the creator of the romantic "Byronic" hero: reckless, sarcastic, "with pleasure drugged," and as irritable as his creator. Just the sight of Byron's dark, heavy-lidded eyes and disdainful mouth convinced his readers that the love affairs described in his poetry were based upon his own amorous adventures.

In fact, there was more to the man described by a youthful friend as "a fat, bashful boy." The son of a gambling, adulterous father who died when Byron was only 3, he was raised by a dour, mean-tempered

Lord Byron wears a Greek turban and jacket in this portrait he commissioned shortly before his death. Determined to help the Greeks defeat the invading Turks, Byron established his own arsenal, drew up plans for a hospital, and lectured the Greeks on military strategy before dying of a fever at Missolonghi. (The New York Public Library Picture Collection)

other creative work, contenting herself with copying her brother's poems in her clear handwriting for his publisher to read. In 1829, some years after William married and moved away, Dorothy Wordsworth suffered a nervous breakdown from which she never recovered.

mother. Lady Byron continually taunted her son because he had been born with a club foot, and the boy became an excellent swimmer and horseman (although he never lost his limp) to discount her criticisms. Byron was educated at Harrow and Cambridge, and like so many English noblemen, he embarked on a grand tour of Europe after graduation. Unlike his peers, however, Byron achieved instant celebrity when his satiric account of his adventures was published in verse form as *Childe Harold's Pilgrimage*.

Byron's influence over manners and attitudes, literary as well as social, was both enormous and long-lasting. *Childe Harold, Don Juan, The Corsair, The Bride of Abydos*, among other poems and plays, were best-sellers, some of them selling out on their first day of publication. His most popular works were titillating, witty, and philosophical. They were set in such exotic climes as Abyssinia (now Ethiopia), Turkey, and Spain and included such scenes as the one in which the hero disguises himself as a woman to sneak into a harem and seduce the sultan's mistress. Throughout his work there was also a dogged search for freedom and escape from convention—the two great Romantic themes.

Byron's fame turned into notoriety after he deserted his wife, the mathematics prodigy Annabella Millbanke, amid rumors of an affair with his half-sister. Becoming an expatriate in Switzerland and Italy, he consorted with such infamous radicals as Percy Shelley before dying while attempting to help the Greeks win their independence from the Turks in 1824. In death, as in life, Byron set the mold for 19th- and even 20th-century artists. "He was irresistible because he had identified himself with . . . fearful forces," wrote Kenneth Clark. "'Let me be,' he . . . [said] to the stormy darkness, 'a sharer in thy fierce and far delight, a portion of the tempest and of thee.'"

"MOODY OUTLAW"

By far the most popular poet of the new century was Lord Byron, whose works were read with "hysterical enthusiasm." Byron was a "moody outlaw . . . haunted by some secret consciousness of guilt" who yet believed in "the possibility of action in the real world." He was the personification of the Romantic artist, too sensitive for the vulgar, materialistic world, and yet highly political. The combination of his good looks, his talent and wit, and his messy love affairs made Byron the first media sensation. It was said that women fainted upon the mention of his name, and his poetry was passed from hand to hand and quoted by the page. The painter J. M. W. Turner so greatly admired Byron that he used passages from his poetry as titles for paintings.

THE NOVEL COMES OF AGE

Not every artist during the Romantic era was as contemptuous as Lord Byron of the established order. King George IV particularly admired another writer of the period, Jane Austen, whose work was both ironic and highly sensible of the value of good judgment and good manners. Austen wrote what became known as "novels of manners." Set in small towns and peopled with upstart farmers, aristocratic landowners, and romantic young women, her novels hinge on subtle social predicaments. Yet the message of *Emma* and *Pride and Prejudice* is one of personal responsibility and integrity.

Austen's brilliance aside, novels were at this time considered the ugly stepchild of poetry. Coleridge refused to believe that reading novels was reading at all; it was instead "a kind of Beggarly day-dreaming." The 19th century saw novels come into their own, and novel reading became the consuming pastime of young women. Even worse, some thought, these ardent readers were writing them. "Everybody scribbles novels," the religious reformer Hannah More lamented, and by everybody she meant women as well as men. The 19th century was the heyday of the woman novelist. Ann Radcliffe, Elizabeth Gaskell, Charlotte Brontë, and George Eliot (the pseudonym of Mary Ann Evans) were just a few of the great women artists who emerged during this century. Byron, however, was harsh in his judgment of women novelists. "Of all bitches dead or alive," he said, "a scribbling woman is the most canine."

FRANKENSTEIN

The novel that incorporates the Byronic hero with the period's simultaneous respect and fear of science is the classic *Frankenstein* by Mary Shelley. The daughter of the feminist Mary Wollstonecraft and the philosopher William Godwin, and the second wife of the poet Percy Shelley, Mary Shelley had an impressive pedigree of artistic accomplishment. *Frankenstein* was begun during her visit with the exiled Lord Byron in Switzerland. As she told the story, she, Percy Shelley, and Byron had each decided to write a ghost story. After Mary Shelley had gone to sleep, her "imagination, unbidden, possessed and guided me, lifting the successive images that arose in my mind with a vividness far beyond the usual bounds of revery." She wrote a novel, born from this dream, that has horrified and thrilled readers for generations. *Frankenstein* is the story of a scientist who breaks the laws of nature by creating life scientifically. The result is a sad and vengeful monster who destroys everything that the scientist loves. *Frankenstein* captures the loneliness and despair of a monster born from man alone, constructed from spare parts like a machine. In her novel, Mary Shelley expressed the Romantic fear of industrialization in a stroke.

The Romantic artists were, in general, both appreciative and fearful of scientific progress. Percy Shelley, who was always experimenting with electricity and weather balloons, so loved speed that it cost him his life: he drowned in an attempt to outsail a storm. William Blake attended Sir Humphry Davy's public lectures on science and experimented in his prints with the latest engraving techniques. Turner devised new mixtures of paint. Coleridge wrote treatises on electricity. But the poet John Keats expressed the artists' fears of a mechanized world demythologized by scientific method when he wrote: "In the dull catalogue of common things / Philosophy will clip an Angel's wings, / Conquer all mysteries by rule and line. . . ." William Wordsworth agreed: "Our meddling intellect misshapes the beauteous forms of things:— / We murder to dissect."

CHAPTER SIX NOTES

p. 64   "the spontaneous overflow . . ." William Wordsworth, preface to
         Lyrical Ballads (London: Methuen, 1959), p. 10.

p. 64   "in the real language of men," Wordsworth, p. 10.

p. 64   "the visible world of tree . . ." John Constable quoted in Kenneth
         Clark, *Civilization* (New York: Harper & Row, 1969), p. 280.

p. 64	"convey a total sense of truth . . ." J. M. W. Turner quoted in Clark, p. 280.
p. 65	"mind-forged manacles . . ." William Blake, *Songs of Innocence and Experience* (Oxford: Oxford University Press, 1986), p. 150.
p. 65	"Princes, the dregs of their dull race . . ." Percy Shelley quoted in White, *Life*, p. 9.
p. 65	"pregnant with religion and poetry," Thomas Grey quoted in Clark, p. 271.
p. 65	"dark, satanic mills," William Blake quoted in White, *Life*, p. 53.
p. 65	"I have very little of Mr. Blake's . . ." Catherine Blake quoted in Johnson, p. 593.
p. 65	"She gave me eyes, she gave me ears," William Wordsworth quoted in Johnson, p. 556.
p. 66	"with pleasure drugged . . ." Lord Byron quoted in Erickson, p. 173.
p. 66	"a fat, bashful boy," quoted in Erickson, p. 74.
p. 67	"He was irresistible . . ." Clark, p. 308.
p. 67	"hysterical enthusiasm," Clark, p. 307.
p. 67	"moody outlaw . . ." Marilyn Butler, *Rebels, Romantics, and Revolutionaries* (Oxford: Oxford University Press, 1981), p. 118.
p. 68	"a kind of Beggarly day-dreaming," Samuel Taylor Coleridge quoted in White, *Life*, p. 155.
p. 68	"Everybody scribbles novels," Hannah More quoted in Erickson, p. 195.
p. 68	"Of all bitches dead or alive . . ." Lord Byron quoted in Erickson, p. 195.
p. 69	"imagination, unbidden, possessed . . ." Mary Shelley, *Frankenstein* (New York: Bantam, 1981), p. viii–ix.
p. 69	"In the dull catalogue . . ." John Keats quoted in W. T. Jones, *Kant to Wittgenstein and Sartre* (New York: Harcourt, Brace & World, 1969), p. 179.
p. 69	"Our meddling intellect . . ." William Wordsworth quoted in Clark, p. 279.

CHAPTER 7

METHODISTS, ABOLITIONISTS, AND FEMINISTS

News of the Reign of Terror—as the years 1793 and 1794 became known in France, when 2,500 French middle- and upper-class citizens were killed by a tribunal of revolutionaries—echoed like a warning shot through the manor houses of England. Fears of a similar revolt by the British lower class prompted some of the gentry to provide a better example for the poor, at least in public.

The push for reform coincided with a conflict within England's hierarchical class system. Newly moneyed industrialists were just beginning to make their way into the middle class. As "mere moneyed men," who made a point of flaunting their wealth, some of these newcomers were not known for their fine manners or good morals. Meanwhile, the shenanigans of the man who would become King George IV in 1820 and of his entourage of "jockeys, bruisers, clowns and whore-masters" further weakened already weak moral standards.

This flattering portrait of George IV, by Sir Thomas Lawrence, depicts the king as both dignified and exceptionally stylish. (The craze for windblown curls and ridiculously high cravats—called "neckcloths"—was pioneered by the king's favorite dandy, Beau Brummel.) What the picture does not reveal is the subject's girth: he weighed at this time more than 300 pounds. (The New York Public Library Picture Collection)

METHODISM AND EVANGELICALISM

The lower classes—the coal miners, factory workers, and field hands—did not go to church at all, and the Anglican church repaid them the favor by ignoring them completely. The lower classes were rarely able to read or write, and they generally had no knowledge of the Bible. It was to them that the Reverend John Wesley preached. An Anglican clergyman who had experienced a religious conversion in 1738, Wesley spent the next 50 years riding on horseback throughout the country, preaching as many as 40,000 sermons to huge crowds of the poor. He emphasized faith over theological learning, and his followers, called Methodists for the methodical regularity of their prayer meetings, were known for their fiery sermons full of hell and damnation. So vivid were some of Wesley's descriptions of hell, that his congregants sometimes fell into fits during his sermons and had to be carried home senseless.

The fervor of Methodism among the lower classes fueled a religious movement nationwide that emphasized conversions, good works, and humanity's sinful nature. Those who believed in church reforms but still considered themselves Anglicans (members of the state church) were called Evangelicals. Some members of the merchant class, however, went further and broke with the Anglican Church altogether, becoming "Dissenters"—members of such pre-existing Protestant sects as the Presbyterians or the Quakers. These denominations stressed what became known as the Puritan work ethic: hard, honest labor; modesty; and thrift. They also promoted education for the working classes and the abolition of slavery.

The Quakers, as members of the Society of Friends were commonly called, were some of the most prominent Dissenters. Many Quaker industrialists owed their financial success to their habit of reinvesting their profits, and to their reputation for honesty and philanthropy. Because Quakers tended to marry within the faith, they formed powerful alliances with other successful Quakers, which furthered many trade and banking agreements.

Many historians believe that it was the influence of Methodism that slowed the spread of revolutionary ideals among the poor. John Wesley, Methodism's founder, and his followers advised the poor to pray rather than involve themselves in politics. Wesley asserted that "the greater the share the people have in government the less liberty, civil or religious, does a nation enjoy."

Some members of the upper classes viewed the religious movement as a political one as well, and indeed there were ways in which the new morality affected politics. For instance, the Evangelical Movement's

HANNAH MORE (1745-1833)

A minor playwright who experienced a religious conversion and turned her "consecrated pen" to morally instructive sermons, pamphlets, and novels, Hannah More was by far the most widely-read author of her day. She was the first person to sell more than a million copies of a book, and in 1812 her *Christian Morals* sold out even before publication.

"Holy Hannah," as she was nicknamed by her critics, was one of the leaders of a group of socially conscious reformers called the Evangelicals. Like many conservatives, she saw the French Revolution as a warning to Britain's aristocracy and began preaching "the need for the privileged to set a good example and for the poor to follow it." More's "religion of the heart," Carolly Erickson wrote in *Our Tempestuous Day*, "appealed to the same yearning for emotional nourishment as did the popular novels that flooded the marketplace, tales of love and loss, Gothic horror, virtue triumphant." Lord Melbourne might complain that "things are coming to a pretty pass when religion is allowed to invade private life," but More's message had found a devoted and devout audience. In earnest, eloquent prose, More admonished her sophisticated, aristocratic audience against worldliness and moral laxity. For the poor, she wrote simple fables aimed at improving morality, and she even founded schools for farm children in rural areas, despite the opposition of the local gentry who believed education would leave the poor "lazy and useless." More and her teachers went so far as to carry out many of the duties once performed by the clergy, who neglected the poor, including baptisms and funerals.

Meanwhile, More's *Thoughts on the Importance of the Manners of the Great to General Society* and *An Estimate of the*

primary spokesman, William Wilberforce, was a member of Parliament and the most famous orator of the day. His political supporters, called the "Saints" or the "praying section of the Tory party," were both politically conservative and ardently philanthropic. They founded societies for the

A typical evening in a crowded laborer's cottage is depicted in this 19th-century lithograph. Hannah More worked night and day to comfort the souls, as well as the bodies, of such people as the ones depicted here, starting schools to educate their children, delivering the eulogy at their funerals, and writing countless stories and ballads to improve their morals. (19th-century lithograph, The New York Public Library Picture Collection)

Religion of the Fashionable World continued to outsell the most popular novels; they were even bought by the government to distribute among the poor. "In every British village," wrote the historian Paul Johnson, "the poor could expect to receive . . . food, old clothes, sometimes a little money, but always a slim printed work by Hannah More." Fame did not turn More's head, however, nor did it make her a feminist. The prefaces of her books were full of shamefaced apologies for her presumption at preaching, and she refused membership in the Royal Society of Literature, believing that it would be inappropriate for a woman to belong.

betterment of the living conditions of the poor; to improve the working conditions of "climbing boys," as chimney sweeps were known; and to help prostitutes, drunkards, homeless children, and refugees.

Wilberforce was aided by Hannah More, a persuasive writer of religious tracts, novels, and ballads. More started a school for poor children and wrote hundreds of instructive religious pamphlets—tracts that the journalist William Cobbett condemned for teaching "people to starve without making a noise . . . and [for] keeping the poor from cutting the throats of the rich." Increasingly, the virtues preached in church were the same as those that factory owners encouraged in their workforce: respect for authority, moderate habits, punctuality, and a love for "the government and laws . . . without asking by whom they are administered."

THE ANTISLAVERY MOVEMENT

Wilberforce and the Evangelicals did much to publicize the gruesome facts of slavery in England's colonies. Working with the Quakers, who were among the earliest abolitionists, they formed societies, started newsletters, and staged public demonstrations. Although it had been illegal to own a slave in England since 1772, the selling of slaves to foreigners from British ports was still an exceptionally lucrative business. One ship carrying 800 slaves from Africa to plantations in the West Indies, South America, or the United States could make a profit of £60,000.

Slavery was the most profitable of all branches of British commerce in the 18th and 19th centuries. It created millionaires in the shipping and cotton-planting industries, and sugar growing and was considered an exceptionally sound economic venture. The slave trade formed a neat triangle of mutual interest and profit. Slave labor in the West Indies and South America produced the raw cotton needed by the British textile industry to make clothing. This clothing produced in Lancashire mills was then sold to Liverpool slavers (slave traders), who carried the textiles to West Africa where they would be traded for "unbroken" slaves (slaves were "broken" or "tamed" after they were sold). These slaves were transported on British ships to the Americas and auctioned off to the owners of, among others, cotton plantations. On the plantations, the slaves would pick cotton to be shipped to the British textile industries while wearing the products of those industries on their backs.

Thanks to the technical innovations of industrialists such as Richard Arkwright and Robert Peel, cotton had become the most valuable agricultural staple in the world, and cotton growing was a booming industry. Much cotton was grown on slave plantations in the West Indies, and Jamaica became the base for England's slave trade. The British also secured control of the West African ports from which slaves were deported to the West Indies and Spain's American empire. The profits were enormous. Slaves sold in the West Indies for five times what they cost in Africa, so the terrible number of people who died in transit (up to 20 percent) scarcely affected revenue. (So important was the slave trade to Britain's economy that as early as 1730 Parliament had granted £10,000 a year to maintain forts on the African coast in order to protect the slavers from local rebellions.)

By 1783, Liverpool had become the biggest port for importing cotton and exporting cotton goods, as well as England's financial base for the slave trade. It was a city where many ill-gotten fortunes were made. "All this great increase in our treasure," remarked Joshua Gee, an 18th-century Englishman, "proceeds chiefly from the labour of negroes in the plantations." It is estimated that Liverpool slavers were responsible for the importation of more than 300,000 slaves to the New World between the years 1783 and 1793 alone. Profits from the sale and exploitation of African slaves were invested in many of Britain's fledgling industries, particularly the iron industry. Slavers were among the few people who could provide the huge sums—as much as £20,000—needed to start an iron foundry. Small wonder that abolition was by no means popular among the many "respectable" people who had made fortunes in the trade of human flesh.

The slavers joined forces with the fabulously wealthy West Indian plantation owners to form a powerful proslavery lobby. Ultimately, however, the abolitionists rallied public opinion to such an extent that Parliament "could not afford to disregard the cry of indignation which had come from every corner of the kingdom." In 1807, after 15 years of nonstop speech making and lobbying, Wilberforce managed to persuade Parliament to pass a law abolishing the slave trade to the British colonies. With that accomplished, he immediately set to work popularizing a bill that would free those people already enslaved.

Finally, in 1825, just one month after Wilberforce's death, slavery was abolished in England's colonies for good.

WOMEN'S RIGHTS

The Evangelicals may have condemned the enslavement of black Africans, but they were profoundly protective of the social hierarchy. Wilberforce and his supporters opposed workers' and women's rights. Consequently, it was many years before women's rights became law or before trade unionism was legalized.

Mary Wollstonecraft was one of the first English women to denounce this discrimination. In her *Vindication of the Rights of Women*, published in 1792, she accused men of controlling women by the use of "simple force." Denouncing her female contemporaries as mere "dependents" trained in "a puerile kind of propriety," she urged reforms that were centuries ahead of their time, such as coeducation for children and women's colleges for the training of doctors, midwives, and businesswomen.

The response to *Vindication* was violently negative; a member of Parliament publicly mocked Wollstonecraft as "a Hyena in petticoats." Most men and women subscribed to a view that was aptly satirized by the novelist George Eliot (Mary Ann Evans): "A man's mind—what there is of it—has always the advantage of being masculine . . . and even his ignorance is of a sounder quality [than a woman's]."

In the 18th and 19th centuries, a woman was classified as either a lady, a servant, or a prostitute. A lady was revered within the home but prevented by custom and by law from owning property, suing for legal redress, opening a bank account, serving in government, or divorcing her husband (her husband, however, could legally divorce *her*). In the case of divorce, a mother had almost no hope of gaining custody of her children. The poet laureate Alfred Lord Tennyson summed the situation up in his poem "The Princess":

Man for the field, woman for the hearth,
Man for the sword and for the needle she;
Man with the head and woman with the heart,
Man to command and woman to obey.

This attitude was directly related to the Industrial Revolution. In the 16th century, women had commonly acted as their husbands' business partners, sharing the work on the manor, on the farm, or in the shop. But as men began working in offices and factories, the women of the middle and upper classes found themselves bound to the care of their appearance, their children, and their home. The historian Asa Briggs categorizes 19th-century women as either "ladies" or "drudges." The former employed "elaborate hierarchies of servants" while the latter did not. "Not all the families who did employ servants were rich," he wrote, "but those who did not employ them were indubitably poor."

Indeed, as the Industrial Revolution progressed, the men of the middle class took great pride in the fact that their wives and daughters were ornamental rather than functional. These women of the "leisured" classes did charity work, cultivated the arts, and entertained; they did not work. If a girl was educated, it was in the "disciplines" of dancing, embroidery, poetry, and singing. She got little or no physical exercise. Miss Elizabeth Bennet, the heroine of Jane Austen's *Pride and Prejudice*, walked three miles to visit her sister who had been taken ill at a friend's house. Despite Elizabeth's good intentions, her sister's friends held Elizabeth in contempt; a real lady would never *walk*.

Some women, however, managed to overcome the social barriers and wrote novels, painted, took photographs, taught, and pursued the sciences. (Sometimes they took bizarre steps to achieve these goals: the popular Victorian doctor James Barry was discovered on his deathbed to have been a woman.) Florence Nightingale transformed the nursing profession; Jane Austen, Charlotte Brontë, George Eliot, and Mary Shelley were popular novelists; and Mary Somerville was a recognized astronomer. But these women were not universally admired for their efforts and achievements. The novelist Anthony Trollope expressed the opinion of most men when he described the ideal woman as one who would "listen much and say but little."

THE NEW WORKING WOMEN

There was one thing that these female achievers had in common; they were members of the middle classes. Women from the working classes rarely managed to achieve distinction; they lacked the necessary financial resources, the education, and the leisure to achieve personal goals.

In the 19th century, poor farmers and artisans had seen their household economies transformed by the factory system. In earlier centuries, the family's income had always been increased by the seasonal wages of the wife and children who worked alongside the husband at harvest time. After the enclosures, women were employed on large farms such as the ones described in Thomas Hardy's *Tess of the D'Urbervilles*, where they weeded and prepared the newly enclosed lands for planting. "It was a vicious circle," historian G. M. Trevelyan contends. "The fact that the husband's wages were not at that time enough to support the whole family forced the wife and daughters into competition with the men for farm service," thereby lowering wages even further.

In the textile mills, however, women were valued as factory workers for precisely the same reasons that they made good farmhands: their hands were quick and their conduct submissive. Women silk workers were paid as much as men, as were particularly skilled women workers in the cotton mills. These women were never considered for managerial jobs, however.

Sexual harassment on the job was commonplace during the Industrial Revolution because it was the first time in British history that women were overseen and paid by men who were not their husbands or sons. The foremen were always male, and there were many cases of coarse, cruel behavior, and sometimes rape, on the large farms and in the factories. Few, if any, foremen were prosecuted in these cases; indeed many people blamed the victims, presuming that all "factory girls" were women of "easy virtue"—or worse. A parliamentary report on the subject asserted that

Not only does [factory work] almost unsex a woman, in dress, gait, manners, character, making her rough, coarse, clumsy, masculine; but it generates a further very pregnant social mischief, by unfitting or indisposing her for a woman's proper duties at home.

The women of the working classes had very few careers to choose from. The daughter of a farmer or a factory worker stayed home and did housework until she was of the age to work beside her parents or "go into service"—that is, become a servant. Those women who came

JOSEPHINE BUTLER
(1828–1906)

*No men, whomever they may be, admire women who
openly show that they know as much on disgusting subjects as
[men] do themselves, much less so those who are so indelicate
as to discuss them in public.*

So wrote a certain Victorian doctor on the activities of Josephine
Butler, a woman who risked her reputation and her liberty to speak
before crowds of hostile men on the immorality of prostitution.

The wife of a minister, Butler led the life of a typical gentlewoman
until one tragic day when her young daughter was killed in a fall.
Butler was heartbroken, and in her grief, she "became possessed with an irresistible desire to go forth, and find some pain keener than my own—to meet with people more unhappy than myself. . . ." She began giving vagrant women any kind of practical help she had at her disposal, and through these women became aware of the huge underclass of prostitutes.

The more prostitutes Butler met, the more she deplored the laws that protected the men who frequented brothels and the madams and pimps

*Josephine Butler's calm determination is
plain in this drawing, completed in 1886 near
the end of her life. Her courage when speaking on street corners before crowds of hostile
men was well known.* (Drawing, 1886, The
New York Public Library Picture Collection)

who lived off the women's degradation. As a woman, Butler could not appeal to Parliament in person, so she began to speak in church halls and on street corners, educating other middle-class women to the realities of child prostitution rings in London and government-sponsored brothels for the Royal Army and Navy. Butler found a champion in John Stuart Mill, a liberal member of Parliament. His eloquence—and the influence of hundreds of women, led by Butler, kneeling in prayer outside Parliament—convinced legislators in 1886 to raise the legal age of consent from 12 to 16 years, and to repeal the Contagious Diseases Act, which had permitted authorities to arrest any woman walking alone in the streets and examine her for syphilis. Butler also campaigned against licensed brothels, traveling more than 3,000 miles, speaking at nearly 100 public meetings, and publishing 38 pamphlets and 6 books in 1870 alone. Her worst enemy, she believed, was not Parliament but the period's attitudes toward women, which portrayed prostitutes as temptresses and men's "straying" as "an irregular indulgence of a natural impulse."

from genteel but poor families—the daughters of clergymen or school teachers, for instance—had the further option of becoming governesses. A governess lived with an aristocratic family and oversaw the children's education until they were ready for boarding school or (in the case of the girls) for marriage. A single woman who was unable to earn a living as a governess, factory worker, or seamstress, or who had been seduced or raped and so could not expect to marry, depended upon her family for support. If that was not possible, she often became a prostitute.

PROSTITUTION

"Imagine London without its 80,000 Magdalens!" wrote the Russian novelist Leo Tolstoy of that city's prostitutes. "How many wives or daughters would remain chaste? What would become of the laws of morality which people so love to observe?" During the 1860s, it was estimated that there were about 9,000 prostitutes working in the city of Liverpool alone, and that 2,000 of these were under the age of 15. England was the world capital of prostitution, partly because land enclosures had brought scores of destitute girls and women to the cities, and partly because of the pedestal upon which "ladies" were placed. The historian Asa Briggs noted that women's sexuality was ignored and denied, and that most men had a "secret life" that involved either a mistress or regular excursions to a brothel.

"The harlot's cry, from street to street / Shall weave old England's winding-sheet*," wrote William Blake, and there was truth in his words. In a society in which divorce was frowned upon, many English men frequented brothels as often as twice a week, bringing venereal diseases—and the madness and death that several of these diseases induced—home to their wives. "The Great Social Evil" as contemporaries called prostitution, proved to be far more difficult to abolish than slavery. Indeed, even the Evangelicals saw prostitution as a necessary institution until a middle-class matron named Josephine Butler showed the world that it was "a practical, hideous, calculated, manufactured and legally maintained degradation of . . . womanhood. . . ."

CHAPTER SEVEN NOTES

p. 71   "jockeys, bruisers, clowns . . ." White, *Life*, p. 139.

p. 73   "the greater the share the people have . . ." John Wesley quoted in Hill, p. 276.

p. 74   "consecrated pen" John Newton quoted in Johnson, p. 382.

p. 74   "the need for the privileged . . ." Johnson, p. 382.

p. 74   "religion of the heart . . ." Erickson, pp. 86–87.

p. 74   "things are coming to a pretty pass . . ." Lord Melbourne quoted in Erickson, p. 86.

p. 74   "lazy and useless" Erickson, p. 89.

p. 74   "praying section of the Tory party" White, *Life*, p. 145.

p. 75   "In every British village . . ." Johnson, p. 382.

---

*A winding-sheet is a sheet in which a corpse is wrapped.

p. 76   "people to starve without making a noise . . ." William Cobbett in White, *Life*, p. 147.

p. 76   "the government and laws . . ." Hill, p. 275.

p. 77   "All this great increase in our treasure . . ." Joshua Gee quoted in Hill, p. 227.

p. 77   "could not afford to disregard . . ." Johnson, p. 327.

p. 78   "simple force" and "a puerile kind of propriety" Mary Wollstonecraft quoted in Elizabeth Longford, *Eminent Victorian Women* (New York: Knopf, 1981), p. 11.

p. 78   "a Hyena in petticoats" quoted in Longford, p. 11.

p. 78   "A man's mind—what there is of it . . ." George Eliot quoted in Longford, p. 13.

p. 78   "Man for the field . . ." quoted in Briggs, p. 243.

p. 79   "elaborate hierarchies of servants" Briggs, p. 242.

p. 79   "listen much and say but little" Anthony Trollope quoted in Longford, p. 19.

p. 80   "It was a vicious circle . . ." G. M. Trevelyan, *Illustrated English Social History*, vol. 4 (New York: David McKay, 1965), pp. 22–23.

p. 80   "Not only does [factory work] almost . . ." quoted in Pike, *Golden Times*, p. 222.

p. 81   "No men, whomever they may be . . ." quoted in Wilson, p. 187.

p. 81   "became possessed with an irresistible . . ." Josephine Butler quoted in Wilson, p. 175.

p. 82   "an irregular indulgence of a natural impulse" Royal Commission Report quoted in Longford, p. 121.

p. 82   "Imagine London without its 80,000 Magdalens!" Leo Tolstoy quoted in A. N. Wilson, *Eminent Victorians* (New York: W. W. Norton, 1989), p. 114.

p. 83   "The harlot's cry . . ." William Blake quoted in Wilson, p. 199.

p. 83   "a practical, hideous, calculated . . ." Josephine Butler quoted in Wilson, p. 198.

THE WAVE OF
REFORM

During the 17th and early 18th centuries, the British government took a very active role in regulating the country's economy. Certain industries were granted government contracts and loans; tariffs were passed to protect the farmers' interests; and trading companies, such as the Massachusetts Bay Company and the East India Company, were given a monopoly on particular trading routes. In the early 1800s, however, many businessmen, influenced by Adam Smith's endorsement of a *laissez-faire* economy, clamored to be allowed to conduct business without any governmental interference. They argued that free trade (no tariffs) and the freedom to set wages, hours, and working conditions would result in a flourishing economy. The government met the industrialists' demands only halfway; a few tariffs were abolished but the Corn Laws were not, and certain monopolies were tolerated. Any bills to restrict working hours or inspect factory conditions, however, were either voted down or, if passed, not enforced.

At the height of the 19th century, an increasingly *laissez-faire* England was acknowledged to have the world's leading economy. Foreigners came from around the world to observe British foundries, factories, markets, and ports. But other sights were not impressive: the industrial cities' slums were among the worst in Europe.

Although Adam Smith had advocated a *laissez-faire* economy in *The Wealth of Nations*, he believed that the government should concern itself with social programs and public works. This aspect of his economic theory was largely ignored, however, because most businessmen saw public education, medical care, and even the establishment of a public water supply as excuses to raise taxes.

THE STRUGGLE FOR PARLIAMENTARY REFORM

Parliament at this time was overwhelmingly *laissez-faire* in philosophy and aristocratic in background. Nearly all its members were great landlords, with just a few industrialists and merchants sprinkled in. This was primarily because elected officials were not paid for their services, and because, to be considered a candidate for office, a man was required to own property worth at least £300. Consequently, the government was dominated by very wealthy men of the Conservative Party (called Tories) who usually voted to protect their own interests. The Liberal Party (also known as the Whigs), which sought regulations and reforms, was in the minority.

This was the situation in June of 1830 when King George IV died at the age of 68, worn out by his extravagant lifestyle. He was succeeded by his middle-aged younger brother, William IV, a gruff navy man with a reputation for liberal thinking. The Whigs, believing that the government should regulate the economy and fund social programs, asked the king to support their push for reforms.

The Whigs proposed a bill to reorganize the election boroughs in order to achieve more equal representation, but it was quickly defeated by the Conservative majority. Riots broke out, sparked by disappointed supporters of the election reforms. In Bristol, a mob broke open the jails and burned down the town hall and the bishop's lavish residence. Taking the riots as the mandate of the people, the Whigs approached William IV and asked him to dissolve Parliament until they could secure more support for their proposals. King William told them that he had "complete confidence" in their "integrity, judgement, decision and experience" and made ready to set out for the House of Parliament. His courtiers attempted to dissuade him, saying that there was not time for the guards to line the streets, but the king would not be stopped. He read the speech of dissolution to the House of Lords and was cheered home by the people of London.

This show of support from the monarch helped the reform cause immensely, and by 1832 the Whigs had gained enough support to pass a parliamentary reform act. This act attempted to correct some inequalities in the voting system by restructuring local governments, making them more democratic, and making certain posts, which had been traditionally "given" to politicians as rewards for political favors, into elected positions. More importantly, it gave the wealthier male members of the middle class the right to vote. This was a step in the right direction, but one which left policemen, postal workers, paupers, and women disenfranchised. Roughly one man in seven had the right to vote in 1832. In 1834, the Whigs went further, introducing a bill allowing Dissenters—as Quakers, Baptists, and members of other Protestant sects were called—to marry in their own churches rather than in the state Anglican churches. Plans to reform factory conditions, child labor laws, the coal-mining industry, and the public health system were in the works, but these improvements faced fierce opposition from the *laissez-faire* Conservatives.

THE DOCTRINE OF DESPAIR

In 1844, Friedrich Engels, the son of a German cotton exporter visited his father's office in the thriving industrial center of Manchester. Unlike most tourists, he toured not only the massive railway station, the fine industrialists' houses, and the new opera hall but also the city's fetid slums. Collaring an English acquaintance, he described with horror the people he had observed living in houses that were as flimsy and dirty as cattle sheds. "I have never seen so ill-built a city," Engels exclaimed. The Englishman replied: "And yet there is a great deal of money made here. Good day, sir." This incident inspired Engels to publish *The Conditions of the Working Class in England,* a study of the living and working conditions of the poor, which helped to awaken European readers to the underside of Britain's prosperity.

The reasons for the terrible conditions in the slums are complex. Improved nutrition, and optimism about the country's continued prosperity, had led to a huge increase in population, from 6.5 million people

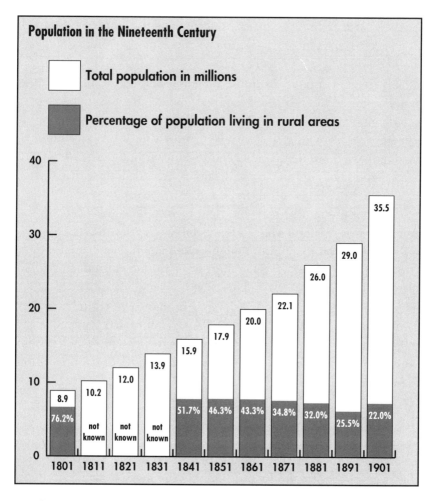

Population in the Nineteenth Century

☐ Total population in millions

■ Percentage of population living in rural areas

8.9	10.2	12.0	13.9	15.9	17.9	20.0	22.1	26.0	29.0	35.5
76.2%	not known	not known	not known	51.7%	46.3%	43.3%	34.8%	32.0%	25.5%	22.0%
1801	1811	1821	1831	1841	1851	1861	1871	1881	1891	1901

Population dramatically increased in Britain during the 19th century, and people living in cities outnumbered those still in rural areas.

in 1750 to almost 14 million in 1830. Many of these people migrated to the industrial cities in search of work, and crowded into dark, dank tenements. Secondly, industrial pollution, faulty sewers, vermin, and little or no medical care allowed such diseases as cholera and typhoid to sweep unimpeded through the slums.

Charitable citizens appealed to the government to improve the workers' living conditions. They published reports of houses built over cesspools, of 30 people having to use the same outdoor privy, of children sleeping in the same bed with their pregnant mother—and their father. Reformers advocated a public water system, flushable toilets, and adequate drains, but their efforts were blocked by the followers of the *laissez-faire* philosopher Thomas Malthus.

Before the publication of the Reverend Thomas Malthus's *Essay on the Principle of Population* in 1798, people had looked forward to an increasing population as a way of sustaining Britain's might and power; "with every mouth God sends a pair of hands" was a popular saying. But Malthus, estimating that the population might double every 25 years, had enlightened these optimists with his "doctrine of despair." Pointing out that the farmland that fed these people could not increase, but in fact would decrease as fields were co-opted for housing, he believed that the result would be famine, poverty, murder, and war— nature's "natural" methods for checking population. To interfere with or attempt to better a poor man's life, Malthus asserted, would merely keep him alive long enough to marry, have a family, and thus contribute to England's overpopulation and ultimate starvation. Therefore, no soup kitchens, no vaccinations, and no charitable handouts should be permitted. "Reformers should . . . allow events to take their inevitable course," he wrote, "and let war, disease, and starvation reap the surplus."

Malthus's *Essay on the Principle of Population* appeared after the factory system had begun to change working people's lifestyles, and many people were converted to its bleak worldview. Poverty and social unrest were growing, but the wealthy classes used Malthus's arguments to absolve themselves of any responsibility for the plight of the lower class.

THE NEW POOR LAW

Certainly, the tough, new Poor Law of 1834 could have been designed by the Malthusians. Under the old Poor Law, known as the Speedenham System, charity had been handed out within church districts (parishes). Small amounts of cash provided by rates (property taxes) were given to poor families that registered with the parish. These amounts, which rose or fell with the price of bread, made up for the loss of earnings of people in cottage industries, and of those who had lost their jobs or been laid off during economic depressions. The downsides of this system were that (1) the poor were not permitted to move from the parish where they were registered, and so were kept from looking for work in other areas, and (2) the payments kept wages down to the lowest level, because manufacturers realized that the parish would make up the difference. But as the price of bread rose, the system became very expensive for tax-paying landowners. Using their considerable powers in Parliament, the landowners legislated the new Poor Law in 1834.

Abolishing the parish payments, the new Poor Law ordered the establishment of workhouses where poor people could be fed and housed in exchange for hard work. Conditions in the workhouses were purposely uncomfortable so as to discourage the "lazy" unemployed. Tea, beer, and tobacco were not allowed, and the sexes were strictly separated—although the sick, the insane, and the violent were all "jumbled together." The underlying philosophy behind the establishment of these gloomy workhouses was that poverty was the result of moral weakness rather than circumstance, and that tough treatment would encourage the poor to "help themselves."

The new Poor Law may have been popular with the members of the middle and upper classes, who approved its cheapness as well as its underlying moral assumptions, but the poor hated the workhouses and nicknamed them "Bastilles," after the infamous Paris prison.

The poor found a champion in the popular author Charles Dickens. His novel *Oliver Twist* tells the story of a sensitive boy born and raised in a workhouse. Oliver Twist experienced firsthand the horrors of that environment, and its alternative: a life of homelessness on the road, begging for scraps of food. When young Oliver falls in with a band of pickpockets, he finds the closest thing to a family he has ever experienced. The point that Dickens stressed was that a vast number of the poor were innocent children, a huge number of whom were orphans.

During the Industrial Revolution, the orphan population exploded as destitute families migrated from farms to cities. Unemployment, disease, and the overcrowding of foul tenements resulted in many children being turned out onto the streets. Dickens described some "thirty thousand naked, filthy, roaring, destitute children" in London. He strove to rescue orphans from the industrial slums—"that vast

CHARLES DICKENS (1812-70)

Charles Dickens was both one of the most popular novelists of all time and one of the age's greatest reformers. The son of a good-natured navy clerk who was always in debt and sometimes in debtor's prison, Dickens received only a cursory education. He was sent to work in a shoe-blacking factory when he was only 12, but his ambition and amazing capacity for hard work got him a position as an office boy in a law firm, then as a reporter of parliamentary debates. Branching into journalism, he began writing witty sketches about everyday life that were published serially in the *Old Monthly Magazine*, among others. So popular were his columns that he was asked to do another series. He came up with *The Posthumous Papers of the Pickwick Club*—a huge hit that made him a celebrity at the age of 24. When Little Nell, the heroine of *The Pickwick Papers*, died, readers were distraught. Dickens received many letters begging him to reconsider her death, and he actually pondered resurrecting her. It was said that Daniel O'Connell, the Irish member of Parliament, was so distressed after reading Nell's death scene, he burst into tears and tossed the offending book out the window.

Charles Dickens greatly enjoyed his huge success. It was said that he radiated good humor and excessive energy. He wrote at top speed; edited newspapers and magazines; traveled extensively; gave public reading tours in America; wrote, produced, and performed in plays; and, in his spare time, drove his friends in old-fashioned coaches.

In his novel *Oliver Twist*, Dickens began his indictment of social injustice, portraying orphaned and destitute children and the criminals who trained them as pickpockets and burglars. When *Oliver Twist* was at the height of its popularity, the young Queen Victoria expressed an interest in reading it. No, no, said her prime minister, Lord Melbourne, she would not enjoy that novel; it was "all about Workhouses, and Coffin Makers, and Pickpockets." But the swelling sympathy for children during the Victorian Age, culminating with the formation of the Society for the Prevention of Cruelty to Children in 1884, owes much to the

Charles Dickens, perhaps the most popular writer in British history, brought the gritty realities of London street life before the eyes of middle-class readers. This photograph from the late 1800s is called The Crawlers—*a slang term for the many London beggars who slept on doorsteps. The woman, worn out by poverty, holds a sleeping baby in her lap.* (The New York Public Library Picture Collection)

many heartbreaking predicaments faced by Dickens's penniless heroes. In *David Copperfield, Bleak House, Great Expectations,* and *Hard Times,* Dickens savagely satirized the hopeless nursery of ignorance, misery and vice"—but there was at that time no viable alternative to slum life other than the workhouse.

CHARTISM

Believing that the working class could provide an alternative to the bleak choice of slum or workhouse if only they could win a role in government, laborers took matters into their own hands. The Chartists, influenced by the theories of the industrial reformer Robert Owen, published a "People's Charter" in 1838. The charter stated six demands:

1. the right of all men to vote (previously only landowners had this right)
2. annual elections
3. vote by secret ballot
4. constituencies (election districts) with equal numbers of voters
5. the abolition of the property qualification for candidates
6. salaries for members of Parliament (so that poorer men could afford to serve in government)

If Parliament refused to support these demands, the Chartists said, there would be a general strike among the factory workers. When Parliament did just that, there were strikes in the West Midlands and Lancashire sections of England, but these were quickly broken up by the authorities. The Chartists' leaders were either arrested or went underground.

Walter Crane's 1886 political cartoon reveals the vampire bat of Capitalism, Religious Hypocrisy, and Party Politics feeding on the blood of a working man. But the angel of Socialism has blown her horn; the laborer will soon awake and, with the angel's help, vanquish the dreadful beast. (Woodcut, from *Cartoons for the Cause*, 1886)

A NEW AGE OF REFORM

In 1837, King William IV died and his 18-year-old niece, Victoria, was crowned queen. A generation would be born, grow old, and die within her 64-year reign. The Victorian Age was a period of unsurpassed power and prosperity for England. It was also a period of public works and reform, as Queen Victoria and her husband Prince Albert impressed upon their subjects the importance of good works as well as good profits.

This new environment brought immediate results. In 1843, a factory bill was passed, reducing the hours of labor for children between 8 and 13 years of age to six and one-half hours a day and requiring attendance at state-supported schools. Many manufacturers objected to the factory law, saying that increased leisure would end in more drunkenness and immorality.

A reform-minded government official named Edwin Chadwick turned his attention to public health and the wretched state of the factory towns. His *Report on the Sanitary Condition of Large Towns and Populous Districts*, published in 1845, provoked a scandal, and in 1848 the Public Health Act established the Board of Health. Such public services as water and the collection of garbage, however, continued to be supplied by private businessmen who disliked the idea of a centralized government authority inspecting their operations. An editorial in the London *Times* summed up the general feeling by saying, "We prefer to take our chance of cholera and the rest than be bullied into health."

Mining proved easier to reform. The conditions in the mines, most of which were owned by aristocrats, were so bad that miners were compared to the slaves working Caribbean plantations. Reformers pushed for a government investigation into the miners' working conditions, and a commission was formed to put together a report on abuses. The report, published in 1842, shocked the public with descriptions of women working knee-deep in water alongside their miner husbands while children loaded coal into tubs or carried back-breaking loads of fuel to the pithead. The report led to the passing of an act forbidding women and children from working underground.

THE ANTI–CORN LAW LEAGUE

Manufacturers who supported free trade—lower prices for wheat would mean cheaper food for their workers and no cost-of-living raises for workers—had formed the Anti–Corn Law League in 1839 and, working with the poor who demanded cheaper bread, now urged an

ROBERT OWEN (1771–1858)

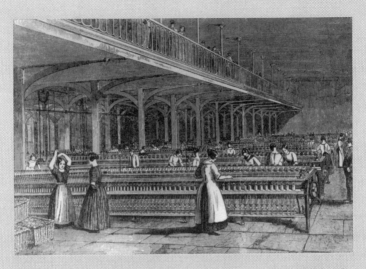

Foremen oversee some Manchester spinners in a "model" mill. In the foreground, two women talk beside baskets of carded cotton. Adequate lighting and ventilation and scheduled breaks were some of the factory reforms that Robert Owen recommended for a happier, more productive work force. (Drawing, from Edward Baines' History of Cotton Manufacture in Great Britain, 1835)

The ideas of a visionary named Robert Owen greatly influenced the history of industrial reform. The owner of New Lanark, a "model" mill in Scotland, Owen worked his way from a poverty-stricken childhood in Wales to a fortune of £60,000 and a reputation for benevolence.

Owen had bought a squalid mill village in Scotland and turned it into a kind of industrial utopia in which workers had good houses, the streets were swept clean by a work detail, and factory rules and regulations were discussed with employees. His mills were well-ventilated, the company store sold fresh foods, and a

THE MECHANICAL AGE

percentage of the profits were reinvested in the community. "I want not to be a mere manager . . . but to . . . change the conditions of the people," he said, and his 2,000 employees, including 500 orphans, were taught to read, write, dance, and sing in the village school.

New Lanark was so impressive—particularly in light of its healthy profits—that 20,000 visitors signed Owen's guest book between 1815 and 1825. The poet Robert Southey toured the new concert, lecture, and ballrooms at the mill, and witnessed a gymnastics lesson that was accompanied by the music of fife players.

Believing that industrialization could bring about progress in sanitation, welfare, work hours, wages, and education, and raise the standard of living for working people, Owen complained that "far more attention has been given to perfect the raw materials of wood and metals than those of body and mind." He began to campaign for factory reform, appealing to other factory managers to take care of their workers "as systematically as they took care of their machinery."

But this was not to be. The Factory Act that was passed in 1819 was a disappointment. Owen's proposals had been disregarded: the maximum hours for a work day were set at 12 rather than 10, and no inspectors were appointed to enforce any of the reforms. Instead, enforcement was left to magistrates, who were often either the mill owners themselves (as in the case of Richard Arkwright) or their cronies.

Owen's idea for reorganizing society into farming communities called "parallelograms"—farming communities of 1,200 people who would live in a single, square building—was even less well-received. However, he did succeed in founding England's first nursery school in 1816 and helped bring about the formation of the Grand National Consolidated Trades Union in 1833. Owen did all he could to help the union's 500,000 members gain wage increases and better working conditions within the factories, but by 1840 the union was dead, weakened by local strikes that failed, infighting, and a fierce and violent opposition by the government.

Still, Owen's belief that human beings could be nurtured as well as frustrated by their environment, that improving working and living conditions would make the workforce more productive, had been confirmed by his experiments at New Lanark. His optimism and idealism continued to foster a desire for fellowship rather than conflict in the cutthroat world of industrial relations.

end to the Corn Laws. Prime Minister Robert Peel made a bold effort toward free trade in 1842 when he introduced a bill reducing the tariffs on wheat and other imports. The aristocratic landowners who supported the Corn Laws successfully blocked the Anti-Corn League until 1845, when a bad harvest brought food shortages.

At the time, Ireland was ruled by the British, and most of its natural resources and crops were exported to England. In 1845, after Britain had imported nearly all of Ireland's grain, a blight spoiled the potato crop—the mainstay of the poor Irish citizen's diet. With no potatoes and no bread to eat, 50,000 people died of famine in Ireland. One million Irish left the country, immigrating to England and the United States.

In Europe, banks were failing in a crisis brought on by overspeculation in railways, and in France, Hungary, and Germany revolutions were brewing. Fears that Britain's hungry poor might revolt if the price of bread went any higher prompted a sudden reversal in Parliament, and the hated Corn Laws were finally repealed in 1846. England was now closer to the free-trade economy advocated by Adam Smith than ever before, and the Victorian spirit of "good works" continued to influence government policy as well. "Too many of us are disposed to place our Golden Age in the past," wrote a reporter for the *Economist* magazine in 1851, but in England "all classes of the community, the humbler as well as the richer, have participated in the blessings" of the Industrial Revolution.

THE MECHANICAL AGE

p. 86 "complete confidence . . ." William IV quoted in Antonia Fraser, *The Lives of the Kings and Queens of England* (New York: Knopf, 1975), p. 294.

p. 87 "I have never seen . . ." recounted in Heilbroner, p. 142.

p. 89 "with every mouth . . ." quoted in R. J. White, *The Horizon Concise History of England* (New York: American Heritage, 1971), p. 175.

p. 89 "doctrine of despair" Heilbroner, p. 91.

p. 89 "Reformers should . . .allow events . . ." Thomas Malthus quoted in Jonathan Miller, *Darwin for Beginners* (New York: Pantheon Books, 1982), p. 112.

p. 90 "jumbled together" and "help themselves" Webb, p. 245.

p. 90 "thirty thousand naked, filthy . . ." Charles Dickens quoted in Eileen Simpson, *Orphans Real and Imaginary* (New York: Weidenfeld and Nicolson, 1987), p. 136.

pp. 90, 93 "That vast hopeless nursery . . ." Charles Dickens quoted in Simpson, p. 136.

p. 91 "all about Workhouses, and Coffin . . ." Lord Melbourne quoted in Briggs, p. 230.

p. 95 "We prefer to take our chance . . ." London *Times* quoted in Webb, p. 289.

p. 97 "I want not to be a mere manager . . ." Robert Owen quoted in Tames, p. 19.

p. 97 "far more attention has been given to . . ." Robert Owen quoted in Tames, p. 20.

p. 97 "as systematically as they took . . ." Robert Owen quoted in Tames, p. 20.

p. 98 "Too many of us are disposed . . ." quoted in Pike, *Golden Times*, p. 38.

THE STEAM
INTELLECT
SOCIETY

Many historians believe that the growth of industry in 18th- and 19th-century Britain was directly linked to the rise of the Dissenting academies—primary schools founded by the Presbyterians, Methodists, Quakers, Jews, and Catholics, who were not permitted to attend Anglican schools. Dissenting academies focused on providing students with a grounding in scientific thought, and Dissenters were among the most educated members of 19th-century society. The inventors James Watt and Matthew Boulton, the engineers Thomas Telford and John McAdam, and the philosopher Thomas Malthus were educated in Dissenting academies, and they credited their interest in science to the lessons they learned there.

EDUCATIONAL REFORM
What made the Dissenting academies so different from Anglican schools was their curriculum: mathematics, history, geography, French, and bookkeeping were taught, as were religious studies. The average upper-class Englishman was wholly ignorant of these subjects.

During the 18th and early 19th centuries, he was most likely tutored at home in reading and writing, then sent at the age of 7 to "public school," a private boarding school that typically offered little more than lessons in ancient Greek and Latin. The food at these schools was meager and badly prepared, and the discipline extremely severe.

After boarding school, young men in England had the choice of studying at one of two universities—Oxford or Cambridge—neither of which was known for its high educational standards at that time. The only qualifications for university admittance until the late 19th-century were that the applicant be male, Anglican, and able to pay the fees. Many students spent their college years doing little more than drinking, gambling, and swimming in the rivers, and the professors (tutors) often enjoyed themselves in the same ways. Tutors were so little respected for their ability to teach that wealthy students often brought their own tutors with them to university. A contemporary reports attending a public debate at Oxford in which "all four participants passed the allotted time in profound silence, each absorbed in reading a popular novel of the day."

The mecca for philosophers, theologians, chemists, social scientists, and doctors in the 18th and 19th centuries was Scotland's Edinburgh University, which, unlike Oxford or Cambridge, admitted Dissenters as well as Anglicans. "The Athens of the North," as Edinburgh University was called, attracted students such as James Watt, who wanted to study chemistry with the famous professor Joseph Black. Black's students were taught the new methods of experimentation and observation that were so important to the development of the 19th century's inventions and discoveries.

As more and more people realized how a knowledge of science was necessary in an increasingly mechanized world, Parliament formed a committee to oversee educational reforms. Sir James Kay-Shuttleworth headed this committee, and it was he who organized a system of 40 colleges for educating a new generation of teachers. Other reforms required university students to pass written examinations before receiving their degrees, a prospect that encouraged serious study. In 1820, England attempted to compete with Scotland by founding London University as a modern university that, like Edinburgh's, offered a practical and useful curriculum. Until the 1850s, London's was the only British university that allowed people of all religions to attend, and it became best known as the center for the study of economics.

Dr. Thomas Arnold, the headmaster of the elite Rugby School from 1828 to 1842, was the most successful educational reformer of the period. Arnold believed that his young students needed to know more about the world than Greek and Latin, so he instituted classes in French, modern history, and mathematics. He particularly stressed the importance of a spartan, morally responsible life, and a restrained "gentlemanly" mode of dress, speech, and expression was rewarded. The British "stiff upper lip" is often credited to the lessons taught by Dr. Arnold, as is the popularity of rugby, the form of football invented at the grammar school.

Dr. Arnold further reformed Rugby School by implementing a system of education known as the "prefectorial method." An upper-classman was chosen to supervise the younger boys' studies; they, in turn, would "fag" for him—make his tea, shine his shoes, and bring wood for his fire. This system was akin to the popular "monitorial method," which was the creation of a reforming body known as the National Society for Promoting the Education of the Poor in the Principles of the Established Church.

THE MONITORIAL METHOD

The monitorial method worked on the principle that "what a boy can learn, a boy can teach." The schoolmaster gave the older boys a lesson. Once he was satisfied that they had learned it, they were made to teach it to the younger pupils. Classes were organized into small groups of monitors and pupils in one large schoolroom. At the ringing of a handbell, the students would begin and end each lesson "like a stage in a process by a large human machine." The benefit of this system was its cost-effectiveness—the boy-instructors were only minimally paid for their services, and fewer teachers meant fewer expenses—but memorization and learning by rote were, of necessity, stressed over understanding.

The poet Samuel Taylor Coleridge admiringly described the monitorial method as a "moral steam-engine," but critics feared that it brought the repetitious atmosphere of the factory to the schoolroom. Charles Dickens, in his novel *Hard Times*, satirized the method in the person of the grim schoolmaster who teaches his students "nothing but Facts." Mr. Gradgrind's question "What is a horse?" elicits the response: "Quadruped. Graminivorous. Forty teeth. . . . Sheds coat in the spring. . . . Hoofs hard."

Dickens feared that imagination and "fancy" were being replaced by so much "useful" knowledge that children were in danger of becoming "parrots and calculating machines." Eventually, the monitorial method's popularity faded and the system was replaced, at the insistence of Sir Kay-Shuttleworth, with the one-on-one tutorial method.

A WORKING-CLASS EDUCATION

Education for the working classes was not forgotten during this period of reform. Already, more members of the working classes knew how to read and write than in the 17th and 18th centuries, when most workers were employed on farms or in the cottage industries. Charity schools had been established in the early 1800s to educate poor children (the Lowood School in *Jane Eyre* is the most infamous fictional example). There were also many Sunday schools, run on charitable contributions, that taught reading, writing, and Bible lessons to factory children (these schools were not necessarily connected to any church, but they were held on Sundays because that was the only day the children were not at work). So that the poor who could read could afford the books they needed, Henry Brougham founded the Society for the Diffusion of Useful Knowledge (parodied as the "Steam Intellect Society") in 1827 and published sixpenny textbooks on scientific knowledge. The author Harriet Martineau even condensed *The Wealth of Nations* into the brief *Illustrations of Political Economy*, which became something of a best-seller.

Adam Smith had foreseen the necessity of a good education for the workers of an industrial society. "The man whose whole life is spent in performing a few simple operations, of which the effects, too, are perhaps always the same, has no occasion to exert his understanding, or to exercise his invention. . . . He naturally . . . becomes as stupid and ignorant as it is possible for a human creature to become," he wrote in *The Wealth of Nations*. Nearly 100 years later, Parliament took Smith's advice and passed the Education Act of 1880, which set up a public school system and made education compulsory for children between the ages of 5 and 10.

THE LUNAR SOCIETY

Other important institutions of learning in the 18th century were the societies of amateur scientists that were popping up all over England. The most famous of these informal groups was the Lunar Society, founded in the 1760s by Erasmus Darwin (the grandfather of Charles Darwin), which brought together some of the greatest minds of the day to discuss various subjects over a pint of beer. The Lunar Society (so-called because it met once a month on the full moon, the light of which made it safer to drive home afterward) has been described as "the intellectual seedbed of the industrial revolution." The engineers James Brindley, Matthew Boulton, and James Watt; the potter Josiah Wedgewood; and the scientist-philosopher Joseph Priestley were all regular members. The Lunar Society examined the chemistry of clays and glazes, and studied surveying, geology, and archaeology—any course of inquiry that could be put to profitable use in industry.

"BANGS AND SMELLS AND BRIGHT LIGHT"

Scientific lectures were also a means of education. Lectures on photography, on laughing gas (used to anesthetize patients so they would not die from the pain of surgery), and on mesmerism (a miraculous "cure" using magnetism) were all the rage in the early 1800s, and they were attended by hundreds of avid enthusiasts.

Sir Humphry Davy, the inventor of the miner's safety lamp, gained a reputation as the greatest lecturer of the period. His talks appealed to a wide audience. Poor poet-engravers such as William Blake attended, as did dukes and duchesses, who watched from private boxes as if they were attending an opera. Davy's lecture series, entitled "Introductory Chemistry," was so successful, it led to lectures on geology, agriculture, and electricity. A master showman, Davy illustrated his talks with "bangs and smells and bright light." His "soda experiment" was spectacular: "the globules flew with great velocity through the air in a state of vivid combustion, producing a beautiful effect of continued jets of fire." But Davy saw science, and chemistry in particular, as more than a "good show" or a way to improve profits in industry. Science was, in his opinion, a means for reducing human

The poor son of a blacksmith, Michael Faraday taught himself chemistry from old textbooks and eventually became the laboratory assistant of Humphry Davy, the greatest scientist of the day. Faraday's experiments with primitive batteries led to the invention of the electric motor (pictured here) and the electric generator. (Thomas Phillips, oil, 1842, The New York Public Library Picture Collection)

misery. The hundreds of people who attended Davy's scientific lectures in London may have come to witness marvels, but their lives would soon be changed by the practical purposes to which his experiments were put.

Davy's assistant, Michael Faraday, was a popular lecturer as well. A self-educated farm boy, Faraday succeeded Davy as president of the Royal Society and became the pioneer of electrical physics. Batteries had been invented in 1800 by the Italian Allesandro Volta, and Faraday used them to isolate the elements sodium, strontium, magnesium, barium, and potassium. In 1831, he rotated a copper disc between two poles of a horseshoe magnet and found that the disc, in turning, picked up an electric current. As simple as it may seem, Faraday had created a dynamo, an electric generator that could be used in motorized engines. (Today, more complicated dynamos convert the energy of coal, oil, or falling water into electricity.)

Faraday, like so many scientists of the period, trusted observation and experimentation rather than mathematical equations and written knowledge. It was precisely this reliance upon physical evidence that precipitated the great crisis of faith of the 19th century.

SURVIVAL OF THE FITTEST

The technical innovations that revolutionized England's industries, not only insured its dominance in the world marketplace, they also enlarged humanity's understanding of the natural world. Discoveries about the physical makeup of the natural world by 19th-century botanists, geologists, and zoologists made people wonder if the Bible's story of creation was really true. Scientists now faced the fearful question, Is God looking after humanity, or is human life beset by forces beyond humanity's control?

Perhaps the most important scientific publication of the 19th century, and one of the most popular—the first edition sold out on the very day it was printed and was the number one topic of conversation for months—was Charles Darwin's *On the Origin of Species by Means of Natural Selection, or The Preservation of Favoured Races in the Struggle for Life*, published in 1859. What Darwin put forth in *The Origin of Species* were two propositions. The first, the idea that the animal species had common origins rather than separate, independent creations, was not new. This idea of evolution had been stated by Jean-Baptiste Lamarck, Robert Chambers, and even Erasmus Darwin. These earlier theories of evolution had included the idea of destinies—predetermined goals to which species strove. These theories, therefore, did not rule out a divine role.

The second proposition of Darwin in *The Origin of Species*, the part that so shocked the world, was natural selection—the theory that creatures changed not according to a divine plan but simply in response to their environment. What later became known as "survival of the fittest" really meant that those individuals best adapted to their environment would survive to reproduce and, thus, pass on their traits to their offspring. (Despite later attempts by politicians and economists to apply Darwinism to society, Darwin himself never meant to suggest that "the fittest" were necessarily superior in any sense other than in their ability to survive long enough to reproduce.)

Unlike his predecessors, Darwin based his theories on solid facts and experimental evidence. It was during an 1835 trip to the Galápagos Islands off South America that Darwin had noticed something that was to influence all his future views. Even though the islands were close to each other and had similar environments, the animals inhabiting each island varied. In fact, Darwin found 13 different species of finches on the islands. This diversity of closely related species sparked Darwin's idea of divergent evolution from a single ancestor in response to the creatures' surroundings.

Darwin stipulated that biological variation, brought about when two species mate, leads to characteristics that eventually become permanent. This idea came as no surprise to stock breeders, who for decades had been selectively breeding cattle, horses, and dogs in order to obtain particular characteristics. But it shocked the British people, particularly after Darwin asserted that, according to skeletal evidence, human beings came from the same genus or family as the chimpanzee and other apes.

Although the scientific community was generally accepting of the theory of evolution, the average British citizen, and even many scientists, were not willing to accept the idea that humans were related to monkeys. To their minds, if one accepted Darwin's ideas, the universe would no longer be ordered according to some divine plan. Suddenly, humanity would be all alone in the world, without the help of a "guiding hand," and Thomas Malthus would have been right—life on earth is just one unending struggle for survival.

CHARLES DARWIN (1809–82)

The popularity of Darwin's groundbreaking treatise *The Origin of Species* had as much to do with the forthright prose with which he explained his theories as with their scandalous content. Darwin had the reputation of being something of an amateur, a gentleman who dabbled in biology and naturalism (the study of nature), and he wrote in a plain, clear style that made his ideas comprehensible to the average reader.

The gifted photographer Julia Margaret Cameron took this picture of Charles Darwin in 1869, when he was visiting the poet Alfred Lord Tennyson. Looking decades older than his 60 years, Darwin was by this time a semi-invalid both respected and reviled for his theory of natural selection. (Library of Science Picture Collection)

Charles Darwin's education was, in fact, unusual for a scientist. His poor showing as a student had made him a disgrace to his family, which, on both his mother's and his father's side, was distinguished by intellectual and financial success (his maternal grandfather was Josiah Wedgewood, the pottery baron, and his paternal grandfather was the poet-philosopher Erasmus Darwin). After failing a course in medicine (the sight of blood made him faint) in his twenties, Charles Darwin was sent to Cambridge to become a clergyman.

Darwin had no interest in becoming a cleric, but he was happy in Cambridge, collecting interesting rocks and fossils and learning taxidermy. In 1832, a friend asked him to become the naturalist on the HMS *Beagle*, which was sailing around the world. For five years the *Beagle* charted the oceans' currents and Darwin explored every landing point, collecting specimens of unusual insects, animals, birds, and rocks. Always a careful observer, he noticed that certain animals, such as armadillos, resembled huge fossilized skeletons that he had seen, but at the time, he couldn't imagine why. This problem was at the root of the question then facing naturalists. If the world was very young—theologians estimated its age at 6,000 years—and if all the plants and animals were the same as they were the day Adam named them in the Garden of Eden, how could one explain the evidence of recently discovered fossils? Were these obviously extinct animals creations God had decided against? And why were there in South America animals that did not exist in England? Had God made separate creations for each continent?

Upon his return to England in 1836, Darwin found that the specimens he had sent home ahead of him had made him a celebrity. He wrote *The Voyage of the Beagle*, a classic travel book, and a treatise on geology, then married his cousin Emma Wedgewood and retired to the country. While compiling his notes from the journey, the first ideas of evolution began percolating in his mind, and Darwin developed his theory of natural selection. A terrible fear of scandal kept him from publishing his ideas, and 15 years passed before *The Origin of Species* appeared.

Darwin's hesitation to publish was not completely unwarranted. Many other scientists had published theories that complemented his own, but *The Origin of Species* was the first book to baldly state what other scientists had only hinted at: (1) that the world had undergone and was still undergoing transformation; (2) that nature provides an unlimited supply of unsolicited, fortuitous hereditary novelties; and (3) that the fertility of nature leads to an unremitting struggle for existence. His conclusion was that in such a struggle, individuals endowed with favorable qualities would survive to reproduce and pass on those qualities to their young. In short, chance—the random variation of genetic combinations— "successfully eliminated any further need for providential action." For Victorian readers, it was as if Darwin had said, "God is dead."

CHAPTER NINE NOTES

p. 101   "all four participants passed . . ." quoted in Heilbroner, p. 46.

p. 102   "like a stage in a process . . ." White, *Life,* p. 164.

p. 102   "moral steam engine," White, *Life,* p. 164.

p. 103   "Quadruped. Graminivorous. . . ." Charles Dickens, *Hard Times* (New York: W. W. Norton, 1966), p. 3.

p. 103   "parrots and calculating machines," Dickens, p. 11.

p. 103   "The man whose whole life is spent in . . ." Adam Smith quoted in White *Life,* p. 162.

p. 104   "the intellectual seedbed . . ." Miller, p. 48.

p. 104   "bangs and smells and bright light," quoted in White *Life,* p. 157.

p. 110   "successfully eliminated any further . . ." Miller, p. 114.

THE EMPIRE
BUILDERS

Look yonder where the engines toil:
These England's arms of conquest are,
The trophies of her bloodless war:
Brave Weapons these.

Victorious over wave and soil,
With these she sails, she weaves, she tills,
Pierces the everlasting hills
And spans the seas.

—"May Day Ode" W. M. Thackeray

In the spring of 1851, 2,000 workmen used 2,300 cast-iron girders, 3,300 pillars, and 800,000 feet of glass to construct an extraordinary building in London's Hyde Park. Three times the length of St. Paul's, London's largest cathedral, the Crystal Palace would be the centerpiece of the Great Exhibition of All the Nations.

In this 1851 lithograph, strollers browse among some 1,500 display cases filled with goods from around the world. More than 6 million visitors toured the Great Exhibition of All the Nations. (The New York Public Library Picture Collection)

THE GREAT EXHIBITION

The idea of a number of businessmen and of Prince Albert, Queen Victoria's consort, the Great Exhibition aimed to showcase the world's technical and industrial achievements. The Crystal Palace—the world's first "prefab" building—was itself an exhibit at the fair. It had been constructed in a record nine months. Surveying the 300,000 panes of glass that sheathed the building's exterior, the art critic John Ruskin sneered that it looked like a huge greenhouse, but many saw the Crystal Palace as a symbol of the British talents for organization and production. The Great Exhibition attracted more than 6 million visitors in the 141 days that it was open, and the businessmen who had funded the enterprise made a huge profit of £750,000 from the sales of tickets and concessions.

The Great Exhibition may have officially exhibited the "Works of Industry of All Nations," but it was truly a celebration of the industrial might of Britain. More than half of the 14,000 displays presented products from England and its colonies. According to a contemporary Englishman, the European exhibits only confirmed that "We can do everything that [Europe] can do—and do it cheaper, and better!" There were a model diving bell (an early submarine), a minutely detailed model of Liverpool, a steam-powered brewery, a working power loom, a flax-crushing machine, and an electroplating machine—all British inventions—for the curious to ogle, as well as such foreign-made goods as finely woven textiles from France, a Colt repeating pistol from the United States, and exquisite lace from Belgium.

What the eight miles of displays made clear to visitors was that the British were using their ingenuity to mass-produce goods and make them affordable to the masses, whereas most European-made goods were luxury items. As a French onlooker remarked: "It is odd that an aristocratic country like England is successful at supplying the people, whereas France, a democratic country, is only good at producing goods for the aristocracy."

"The British made what the world wanted and needed," wrote the historian R. K. Webb, and it did that by mechanizing existing industries and creating new ones. Farming, for instance, had come a long way since Jethro Tull first made his agricultural experiments. Planting and harvesting had been revolutionized by steam-powered threshing machines and reapers. The making of machine tools, used to fix those reapers and other machines, had recently become a booming business in and of itself. In other countries, a factory might sit idle for days while the owner tracked down a mechanic with the right tools and spare parts to fix its machines. The British, however, could now fix their broken machinery with little difficulty.

The British invention and improvement of machine tools, and the standardization of threads on screws and bolts, led to a new kind of precision in machinery that not only increased efficiency but made it easier for British industries to mechanize. By the end of the 19th century, the only major industries in England that were still done by hand were cutlery, tailoring, and dressmaking.

THE BRITISH EMPIRE

Prince Albert addressed the crowd at the opening ceremony of the Great Exhibition. "The products of all quarters of the globe are placed at our disposal," he said. "And we have only to choose that which is best and cheapest for our purposes. . . ." His words had a special meaning for his subjects; they knew that much of Britain's wealth came from its far-flung colonies. During the Industrial Revolution, Britain had been able to pursue an imperialist foreign policy of annexing countries that were less industrialized. Through the military conquest of poorer, less powerful nations, Britain was able to command the cheap raw materials its industries needed. The low prices paid for colonial resources allowed the British to make their products cheaply and thus outsell all foreign competitors. The colonies also provided markets for England's surplus goods.

The British had begun their empire building early. The 16th-century navigator Richard Hakluyt had commended England for excelling "all the nations and peoples of the earth" in "searching the most opposite corners and quarters of the world and . . . in compassing the vast globe." By the 18th century, navigation had become a scientific procedure with the invention of the compass and the sea quadrant (the work of the Englishman John Davis); explorers had sailed to the Americas and to Russia, Africa, India, Morocco, Japan, and China. Intrepid British entrepreneurs had established trade routes, plantations, and markets.

By 1700, the British had trading posts in North America, India, and the West Indies, and along the eastern coast of what is now the United States. By 1800, Britain had lost the 13 American colonies but had gained control of Canada and planted settlements in Australia and New Zealand.

The British permitted their colonies a certain degree of self-rule, and England's parliamentary and legal systems were transplanted in many of its colonies. Trading companies for doing business with the colonies were chartered by the British government, and many such companies, through diplomacy or warfare, acquired monopolies on certain colonial exports—monopolies that gave the companies great power and wealth. The most powerful of these was the East India Company.

The East India Company

For nearly 260 years, the East India Company brought the spices, textiles, jewels, and rare oils of the East, and the teas and crockery of China, to British markets. Founded in the 17th century, the East India

Company competed with Portuguese, Dutch, and French traders to gain control of the rich Indian markets. After the Mogul Empire that had ruled India for about 200 years began to break up in the 18th century, and regional disputes threatened to result in civil war, British and French traders began to intervene in Indian politics, each group hoping to bring about a commercial climate that would favor its interests.

In 1757, Robert Clive, an administrator of the East India Company as well as a military leader, led 3,200 troops against a force of 50,000 French and Indian allied troops at Plassey in India. Clive's near-miraculous victory won the company Bengal, the richest province in India, and increased the company's profits by £2 million a year. Granted the right to tax the native peoples in order to maintain British forts, the East India Company wielded unlimited power in India for half a century.

In 1857, the embittered Indian army incited the bloody Sepoy Rebellion, which was quelled with great losses to the Indians in 1858, the same year that the British government purchased control of India from the East India Company. In 1876, Queen Victoria became the

An aging Queen Victoria, under the watchful eye of her Indian servant Abdul Karim, goes through her official papers outdoors. The many boxes on her makeshift desk give a hint of the royal responsibilities in ruling a vast empire. (Carbon print by Hills and Saunders, 1893, The New York Public Library Picture Collection)

empress of the vast Indian subcontinent—"the brightest jewel in the imperial crown."

The China Trade

Profit was the motive that drove the British merchants to establish more and more colonies. As British outposts came under attack by the native populations, the British army was again and again called on to defend the merchants' interests. In this way, Britain gained its empire. A good example of the process was Britain's relationship with 19th-century China.

In 1839, the son of the emperor of China died. Like so many millions of Chinese, the son had been addicted to opium. The importation of this deadly drug into China was illegal, but British merchants had been ignoring the laws and were supplying tons of opium to Chinese smugglers. The grieving emperor decided to put a stop to this illicit trade. He ordered that more than 20,000 chests of opium, sent by the East India Company from India, be dumped into the sea.

The British were enraged. The money from their opium trade had allowed them to buy the ivory fans, the porcelain vases, the teas and silks that British citizens so admired. The British also realized that if the Chinese were allowed to close the port of Canton (the only Chinese port open to foreign traders) to British merchants, England would lose a huge market for its manufactured goods. Britain declared war on China, and, after three years of war, defeated that country in 1842. A victorious Britain then annexed the island of Hong Kong and forced China to open four more ports to European trade. In the second Opium War (1856–60), France joined with Britain to force China to open even more ports. Soon China's coal, iron, minerals, and luxury goods were being exported by the ton, and Britain was selling opium and other goods to millions of eager Chinese consumers.

"The Sun Never Sets on the British Empire"

The empire was extended still further between 1870 and 1898, when Britain brought more than 4 million square miles of territory and 88 million people under its rule. By the end of the 19th century, the British Empire stretched from New Zealand to Canada, from the Falkland Islands to Ceylon and the Malay Peninsula, from the Caribbean to Australia, and from Hong Kong to the Cape Colony of South

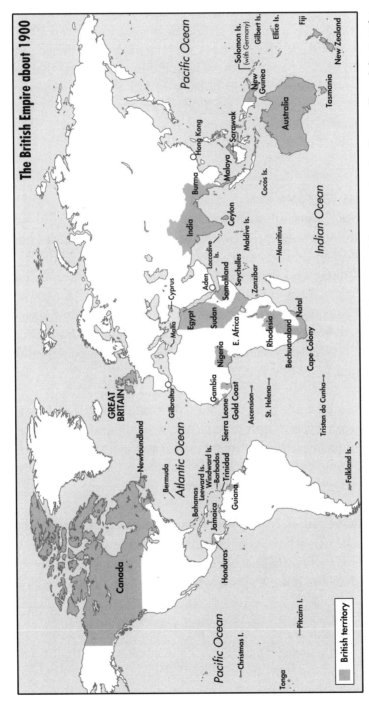

The British Empire about 1900

Britain's empire in the 1890s covered numerous territories around the world. The extent of their control and influence allowed the British to gather raw materials from their colonies, transport the goods on protected waterways, and bring the cargo home to their factories.

Africa—over a quarter of the earth's surface. Huge quantities of raw materials were exported to England, which in turn exported machinery, skilled workers, and manufacturing techniques to the colonies, essentially bringing the Industrial Revolution to the world. Railways and cotton mills were built in India; gold and diamond mines were excavated in Africa; and in 1869, the Suez Canal was built in the Middle East, a feat of engineering that shortened Europe's route to India by about one-third.

DIVISIONS AT HOME

With Britain's wealth and power came certain moral problems. Corruption was widespread within the colonies, and most British citizens turned a blind eye to the inhumane conditions in African diamond mines and on Indian tea plantations. Dishonest colonial officials who accepted bribes for allowing a variety of abuses were rarely prosecuted. Many company administrators made huge fortunes in India, and some of them bought their way into British politics. "The riches of Asia have poured in upon us," a contemporary complained,

> and have brought with them not only Asiatic luxury, but I fear, Asiatic principles of government. Without connections, without any natural interest in the soil, the importers of foreign gold have forced their way into parliament by such a torrent of private corruption as no [one] could resist.

As British territorial gains created millionaires at home, the divisions between the rich and the poor became immense. For England's ruling class, the pursuit of wealth and power had become an end in itself, an attitude that bore bitter fruit when upper and lower classes clashed.

Organized Labor

Throughout the late 19th century, the vast majority of British workers had voted for the Liberal Party because the Liberals seemed interested in their welfare. Yet many workers felt that they should organize their own party to win even greater benefits. This feeling intensified as trade unions grew in size.

Beginning in the 1830s, several laws were passed to improve working conditions, and in the 1870s, strikes were made legal and collective bargaining was recognized. Despite these advances, unskilled workers made little progress in unionization until the dockworkers' strike of 1889. By avoiding violence, the dockworkers won not only their strike but the sympathy of important statesmen and the public. Many workers who had seen how the union had helped the dockworkers improve their working conditions now joined unions. More and more people were rejecting Malthus's *laissez-faire* philosophy and calling for social programs to help the poor, and for such government "interferences" as health inspectors and public sanitation.

In *The Wealth of Nations*, Adam Smith had asserted that no society could flourish and be happy if most of its citizens were destitute and miserable. During the later years of the 19th century, it seemed as if the working classes had reached a kind of understanding with their employers. In 1848, Karl Marx, the founder of the political philosophy known as communism, had looked at the state of Britain's industrial relations and predicted the quick demise of free trade, privately owned factories, and the British economy. But, as it happened, an 1886 Royal Commission report showed that working conditions were actually improving as the economy flourished. Wages were higher and working hours shorter than ever before. In fact, in a letter he wrote to Marx, Friedrich Engels lamented that "the English proletariat is . . . becoming more bourgeois."

The New Leisure

As trade unions won concessions from the industrialists, the middle classes were able to afford such luxury items as telephones (invented in the United States in 1876 by Alexander Graham Bell), phonographs (invented by the American Thomas Edison in 1877), automobiles (invented by Edward Butler, a British farmer, in 1888), and, cameras—the latest craze. Leisure was a newfound pleasure, and bicycling, bathing at the seashore, and team sports filled the new "English weekends." The 64 years of Victoria's reign became known as the Age of Complacency.

JULIA MARGARET CAMERON
(1815-79)

The first cameras to reach England in the 1830s were primitive machines. In order for the photograph to be in focus, the subjects had to remain perfectly still for as long as 10 minutes while the negative was exposed. Consequently, during the first few decades of their use, cameras produced portraits that were unflattering, artificial-looking, and unrevealing. But this was to change with the work of one woman, Julia Margaret Cameron, who received a camera as a gift in 1864, when she was 48 years old.

She converted her coal cellar into a darkroom, and quickly mastered the process of developing pictures. And she tirelessly photographed her servants, her neighbors, and the people who visited her large house on the Isle of Wight in the English Channel. Producing more than 500 photographs a year between 1863 and 1875, Cameron took photographs that were unlike any others of the period. It was said that she saw into her sitters' souls.

Cameron may have been a remarkable photographer—the art critic Roger Fry called her one of the greatest Victorian artists—but she was also an eccentric born into a large and peculiar Anglo-Indian family. Her sitters' expressions, her biographer wrote, were often ones of "absolute incredulity that anyone could be quite so extraordinary as the lady behind the camera." Cameron spent many hours photographing her neighbor, the poet Alfred Lord Tennyson, and it was at his house that

WAR

The Age of Complacency was to end in war. As Britain, confident of its power around the world, became more arrogant in its treatment of native peoples and more aggressive in its competition with other European imperial powers, nationalism grew at home. As England competed with the highly industrialized Germany, France, and Belgium to annex even more colonies and to find more markets for its goods, war became inescapable. The poet Rudyard Kipling summed she was introduced to the Italian statesman Giuseppe Garibaldi. When the effusive photographer fell to her knees and attempted to kiss his hand, Garibaldi, mistaking this woman with black curly hair, dangling earrings, and hands stained black by developing medium for a Gypsy, shooed her away. "Waving her filthy hands," wrote A. N. Wilson, Cameron defiantly told the man: "This is Art, not Dirt."

Cameron pioneered the use of the close-up, exposing, for instance, the sad look in the eyes of the historian Thomas Carlyle, and the quiet menace in Tennyson's expression. The backgrounds of her photos were often blurred, with light emanating from the person's clothes or filtered through their hair. Particularly popular at the time were her tableau photos, in which she illustrated poetry by using young women costumed as Guinevere or guardian angels. Her work was highly regarded and was exhibited in Dublin, Berlin, London, and Paris, helping to promote the "camera mania" of the late Victorian Age.

So beautiful were some of her pictures that they provoked unusual reactions. One morning a young man rang the doorbell of the Cameron house and announced: "I have come to ask for the hand of your housemaid." He had seen the girl's portrait in an exhibit of Cameron's work. Incredibly, the pretty servant accepted her suitor's offer and they were married—to Cameron's great delight. "It was a marriage of bliss," she said, "with children worthy of being photographed, as their mother had been, for their beauty."

up England's "jingoistic" attitude at the end of the 19th century with the verse: "We don't want to fight, but by jingo if we do, / We've got the ships, we've got the men, we've got the money too!"

The Crimean War, which Britain fought from 1853 to 1856 to defend its interests in the Balkans and the Middle East against Russian expansionism, was only the beginning of a series of conflicts around the world. These included the disastrous Boer War, which was fought from 1899 to 1902 against the Dutch-born, German-armed white settlers in southern Africa. The British and their allies won the Crimean War, but at a great price in soldiers and money; the Boer War deteriorated into guerrilla fighting and the British internment of Boer women and children in prison camps. Ultimately, the Boers accepted British rule, but the war proved a financial and moral setback for Britain.

THE IMPERIALIST LEGACY

Nineteenth-century imperialism had wrought great changes. When Britain and other European powers moved into exotic lands, they brought not only western products but new ideas about religion, government, and art. Sanitation, education, better transportation and communication, and scientific methods of agriculture and industry were introduced around the globe. The imperialists, in turn, found themselves influenced by their colonists. Eastern and Indian philosophies, Canadian furs, Chinese medicinal plants, and African art had as great an effect on Britain as the introduction of such colonial products as rubber, oil, silk, tin, and tropical fruits.

As the 19th century came to a close, British threshing machines were harvesting crops in China and Africa; British-made locomotives criss-crossed India; Caribbean children read Wordsworth's poems in British-run grammar schools; and English matrons, dressed in Indian silks, sat on furniture carved from African mahogany, and served Chinese tea to their guests. The ideas of Adam Smith and the inventions and reforms of a generation of diligent, progressive men and women had altered the world forever.

CHAPTER TEN NOTES

p. 113 "We can do everything that [Europe] can do . . ." quoted in Pike, *Golden Times*, p. 22.

p. 113 "It is odd that an aristocratic country . . ." quoted in Briggs, p. 189–190.

p. 113 "The British made . . ." Webb, p. 281.

pp. 113–114 "The products of all quarters of the globe . . ." Prince Albert quoted in Briggs, p. 189.

p. 114   "all the nations and peoples . . ." Richard Hakluyt quoted in Briggs, p. 160.

p. 116   "the brightest jewel . . ." White, *Horizon*, p. 185.

p. 118   "The riches of Asia have poured . . ." quoted in White, *Horizon*, p. 188.

p. 119   "the English proletariat is . . . becoming . . ." Heilbroner, p. 144.

p. 120   "absolute incredulity that anyone . . ." Wilson, p. 222.

p. 121   "Waving her filthy hands . . ." Wilson, p. 222.

p. 121   "I have come to ask . . ." quoted in Wilson, p. 216.

p. 121   "It was a marriage of bliss . . ." Julia Margaret Cameron quoted in Wilson, p. 216.

p. 121   "We don't want to fight, but by jingo . . ." Rudyard Kipling quoted in Briggs, p. 222.

THE INDUSTRIAL
SPIRIT IN DECLINE

In the early days of the 20th century, it was becoming clear that England's economy was losing ground. The British economy was very different from what it had been in the early 1800s. Family businesses had become corporations, and the largest of these had grouped together to influence government. Efficiency experts had been brought in to set quotas for production—to the disgust of the workers. Meanwhile, a new class of skilled, educated employees— called "white collar" workers—had been trained to become typists, clerks, salespeople, and managers in these corporations.

Also, there had been a steady worsening of the relationship between factory owners and their workers. While the industrialists and landowners now were more affluent than ever, spending their fortunes on mansions, huge staffs of servants, and fast automobiles, the poor were getting poorer. The trade unions organized fierce strikes during the years 1910–14, and Britain seemed on the verge of industrial collapse. Women were agitating for the right to vote, and Ireland was on the verge of civil war. The newly powerful trade unions were opposing technical innovations that might cost their members their jobs. Consequently, newer and more efficient German and American manufacturers were able to flood the world market with inexpensive goods.

In 1914, England became involved in World War I. The use of new mechanical weapons, such as airplanes and machine guns, and of poisonous mustard gas resulted in millions more people being involved in this war than any previous international conflict. By the time the war ended in 1918, Europe had been devastated and Britain's industrial preeminence curtailed.

"England used to be like a big international firm," an Englishwoman recently told a reporter, "and now, well, sometimes it seems as if the country has just gone into liquidation." Britain is now seen as the prime example of a post-industrial society, the first mechanized society to face massive unemployment, a dearth of natural resources, and the legacy of industrial pollution. As other industrialized nations, such as the United States, reach a similar point in their economic cycle, they look to Britain for ideas for rejuvenating their productive powers while maintaining social programs.

In an essay, the historian Arnold Toynbee wrote that "the more we examine the actual course of [the Industrial Revolution], the more we are amazed at the unnecessary suffering that had been inflicted upon the people." Without diminishing the horrors of the industrial workplace and the displacement of thousands by land enclosures and new inventions, it can also be said that Britain's Mechanical Age was a time of remarkable promise, optimism, imagination, and change on a grand scale. Agriculture gave way to industry, the aristocracy to the middle class and a powerful working class movement. Freedoms were gained—and lost—but the breathtaking pursuit of progress and advancement continued, as it continues today, both in Britain and around the world.

EPILOGUE NOTES

p. 125   "England used to be like a big international firm . . ." William E. Schmidt, "D-Day to Celebrate, and Britain's in the Mood," *New York Times*, May 31, 1994.

p. 125   "The more we examine the actual course . . ." Arnold Toynbee quoted in Hill, p. 265.

CHRONOLOGY

1760 • George III is crowned king of England.

1769 • James Watt's steam engine is patented.

1773 • The Boston Tea Party: American colonists protest against the East India Company's monopoly of tea exports to America.

1776 • Adam Smith's *An Inquiry into the Nature and Causes of the Wealth of Nations* is published. The Declaration of Independence is signed in Philadelphia.

1781 • The American Revolution ends.

1789 • The French Revolution begins.

1791 • Thomas Paine's *The Rights of Man* is published.

1793 • Mary Wollstonecraft's *Vindication of the Rights of Women* is published. Britain enters the French revolutionary wars in Europe. England experiences a commercial depression.

1798 • The Reverend Thomas Malthus's *Essay on the Principle of Population* is published. A tax of 10 percent on incomes over £200 is introduced.

1799 • Trade unions are suppressed. Napoleon is appointed first consul in France.

1799–1801 • England has a commercial boom.

1801 • Ireland is united with England. The first British census is taken.

1802 • Peace is achieved with France. Peel introduces the first factory bill.

1803 • Britain declares war on Napoleonic France.

1805 • The Battle of Trafalgar. Britain's General Horatio Nelson defeats the French and Spanish fleets.

1809–10 • England experiences a commercial boom.

1811 • England has an economic depression. "Luddite" disturbances occur in Nottinghamshire and Yorkshire. George III is declared incurably mad; his son George, the Prince of Wales, is made prince regent.

1812–14 • The War of 1812 with the United States occurs.

1815 • The Battle of Waterloo: Napoleon is defeated by the Duke of Wellington's troops. The Corn Law is passed.

1819 • The Peterloo massacre occurs.

1820 • George III dies; George IV is crowned king.

1825 • Trade unions are legalized.

1830 • George IV dies; his brother, William IV, is crowned king. The Liverpool and Manchester Railway opens.

1832 • The Great Reform Bill restructures representation in Parliament.

1833 • The Factory Act limits child labor.

1834 • Slavery is abolished in the British Empire. Parish workhouses are instituted. Robert Owen founds the Grand National Consolidated Trade Union; action by the government against "illegal oaths" in unions results in the failure of the Grand National Trade Union and the transportation (deportation to Australia) of six union leaders.

1835–36 • A commercial boom is sparked by the "little" railway mania.

1836	•	Chartist movement is started.
1837	•	King William IV dies; Victoria is crowned queen.
1838	•	The "People's Charter" is drafted.
1839	•	The Chartist riots occur; Anti-Corn Law League established.
1839–42	•	First Opium War with China.
1840	•	The Penny Post is instituted.
1842	•	Mines Reform Act becomes law. Edwin Chadwick issues his report on sanitation.
1844–45	•	Railway mania: massive speculation and investment lead to the building of 5,000 miles of track. The potato famine begins in Ireland.
1846	•	The Corn Laws are abolished.
1847	•	The Ten Hours Act limits the workday.
1848	•	Revolutions occur in Europe. The Public Health Act becomes law.
1851	•	The Great Exhibition of All the Nations is held in Hyde Park, London.
1853–56	•	In the Crimean War, England defends European interests in the Middle East against Russia.
1856–60	•	The second Opium War.
1858	•	The Indian mutiny and the India Act end the East India Company's control of India.
1859	•	Charles Darwin's *On the Origin of Species by Means of Natural Selection, or The Preservation of Favoured Races in the Struggle for Life* is published.
1875	•	Britain takes control of the Suez Canal from France.
1880s–1890s	•	Cecil Rhodes annexes African territory.
1899–1902	•	The Boer War takes place in southern Africa.
1901	•	Queen Victoria dies; her middle-aged son, Edward VII, is crowned king.

FURTHER READING

NON-FICTION BOOKS

Clare, John D., ed., *Industrial Revolution* (San Diego: Harcourt Brace, 1994). This young-adult book covers the history of the Industrial Revolution throughout western Europe and the United States. Its main theme is that the changes that were made did not improve the lives of most workers.

Dale, Rodney, *The Industrial Revolution* (New York: Oxford University Press, 1994). A short volume for younger readers, this book tells a brief history of the mechanical advancements of the Industrial Revolution. It is a part of Oxford's Discovery and Inventions series.

Erickson, Carolly, *Our Tempestuous Day: A History of Regency England* (New York: William Morrow, 1986). A witty, engaging description of life during the Regency, including thumbnail biographies of the major figures of the period.

Fanning, Leonard M., *The Fathers of Industries* (Philadelphia: Lippincott, 1962). Fanning devotes each chapter to a different inventor, filling in the biographical details and explaining how their inventions worked, how they were initially manufactured, and how they were improved and modernized to serve a purpose today.

Langford, Paul, and Christopher Harvie, *The Eighteenth Century and the Age of Industry* (Oxford: Oxford University Press, 1992, paper).

A factual account of the Industrial Revolution, complete with tables, graphs, and helpful maps.

Langley, Andrew, *The Industrial Revolution* (New York: Viking Children's Books, 1994). Part of Viking Children's See Through History series, this book teaches younger readers the effects of the Industrial Revolution on western Europe and the United States.

Lines, Clifford, *Companion to the Industrial Revolution* (New York: Facts on File, 1990). With alphabetical entries for all the major figures, ideas, inventions, and political events of the Industrial Revolution, this indispensable reference book is the perfect place to find a concise answer to most questions on the subject.

Longford, Elizabeth, *Eminent Victorian Women* (New York: Knopf, 1981). A beautifully illustrated collection of short biographies of some distinguished women of the Victorian Age. Whether of artists, doctors, reformers, or mystics, the lives presented here make for fascinating reading.

Miller, Jonathan, *Darwin for Beginners* (New York: Pantheon Books, 1982). A cartoon-filled explanation of evolutionary theory, invaluable for anyone who wants to learn about 19th-century intellectual thought and Darwin's life and works.

Pike, E. Royston, *"Hard Times": Human Documents of the Industrial Revolution* (New York: Frederick A. Praeger, 1966), and *Golden Times: Human Documents of the Victorian Age* (New York: Schocken Books, 1972). These selections from the actual documents, newspaper articles, biographies, and editorials of the time give the reader an eyewitness view of the Industrial Revolution.

Quennell, Marjorie, and C. H. B. Quennell, *The History of Everyday Things in England*, vols. 3 and 4 (New York: G. P. Putnam, 1961). If you find yourself wondering just how the spinning jenny worked, or how the first locomotives used steam power, or what a water closet looked like, look no further than this helpful illustrated series. The authors are so knowledgeable about the mechanics and history of the inventions they describe, they can explain the workings of everything from suspension bridges to telegraphs.

Tames, Richard, *Radicals, Railways and Reform: Britain 1815–51* (London: B. T. Batsford, 1986). A brief but informative look at the key figures of the Reform period. Illustrated.

Trevelyan, G. M., *Illustrated English Social History*, vol. 4 (New York: David McKay, 1965). A concise history of the Mechanical Age is given in the later chapters. Color illustrations.

FICTION AND POETRY BOOKS

Austen, Jane, *Pride and Prejudice* (New York: Penguin, 1974, paper), and *Emma* (New York: W. W. Norton, 1972). Two of the best-loved novels of the 18th century, Austen's works are witty, ironic, and acutely described.

Brontë, Charlotte, *Jane Eyre* (New York: Random House, 1943), and *Shirley* (Oxford: Oxford University Press, 1991, paper). *Jane Eyre* is the better novel, and its tale of the life of a governess who falls in love with her employer has become a classic fairy tale. Like *Shirley*, however, it reveals a keen social sense and firm opinions about the social problems affecting England during the late 18th and 19th centuries.

Byron, Lord, *Don Juan* (New York: Random House, 1949). Byron's amorous, cynical hero can still make modern readers feel the fervor and admiration that greeted this book-length poem when it was first published in 1823.

Dickens, Charles, *Hard Times* (New York: W. W. Norton, 1966, paper), and *Oliver Twist* (Oxford: Clarendon, 1966). Funny, imaginative, and heart-wrenching tales of industrial England.

Eliot, George, *Middlemarch* (New York: Penguin, 1981, paper). The England of the Reform period is amusingly illustrated by a cast of characters that includes Dissenters, social-climbing industrialists, gambling clerics, Evangelicals, and Whigs.

———, *Silas Marner* (New York: Harper & Row, 1965). A portrait of a miserly cottage weaver in pre-Industrial England. The relationship between the village and the lord of the manor is entertainingly illustrated with some scenes in the local pub. The local people's suspicions about Silas Marner because he is a Dissenter help modern readers understand the 18th-century qualms about the new Protestant faiths.

Keats, John, *Poetical Works* (Oxford: Oxford University Press, 1956, paper). The collected works of a great Romantic poet. Although he died at the age of 26, Keats is considered one of the greatest poets to write in English.

Shelley, Mary, *Frankenstein* (New York: Bantam, 1981, paper). More frightening than the movie version, this tale of alienation and bloody revenge illustrates the Romantic response to scientific progress.

Shelley, Percy, *Complete Poetical Works* (Oxford: Oxford University Press, 1989, paper). Shelley is the most political, and perhaps the most influential, of the Romantic poets. His work is both lyrical and nonconformist.

Tennyson, Alfred Lord, *Poems* (New York: Houghton Mifflin, 1958, paper). The selected works of the Victorian poet laureate. His poems communicate the attitudes of the age: the fears, enthusiasms, prejudices, fantasies, and sentiments. "The Charge of the Light Brigade," about an incident during the Crimean War; "Idylls of the King," a retelling of the King Arthur story; and "In Memoriam," the heartrending elegy to his best friend, are unforgettable.

Wordsworth, William, and Samuel Taylor Coleridge, *Lyrical Ballads* (London: Methuen, 1959). The book that launched the Romantic Movement in England. The introduction is as famous as the poetry, but read "The Idiot Boy" or "The Female Vagrant" to get a sense of Wordsworth's ideas in action, and Coleridge's "The Rime of the Ancient Mariner," one of the strangest, most affecting ballads ever written.

THE MECHANICAL AGE

INDEX

factory system 6–8, 16, 51, 80, 89, 102
Faraday, Michael *105,* 106
firedamp 30, 31
Flood, Frederick 54
fly shuttle 16
Frankenstein **68–69**
Franklin, Benjamin 2
French Revolution 4, 20, 53, 60, 63, 74
Fry, Roger 120
Fulton, Robert 44

Gaskell, Elizabeth 68
Gee, Joshua 77
George III, king of England 4, 11, 17, 54, 59
George IV, king of England 54, 59, 68, 71, 72, 86
Godwin, William 69
Grand National Consolidated Trades Union 97
Grand Trunk Canal 41–42, 43
Great Eastern 45
Great Exhibition of All the Nations **111–13**
Great Expectations 92
Great Reform Bill 61
Great Western 45

Hakluyt, Richard 114
Hard Times 92, 102
Hardy, Thomas 80
Harris, Betty 28
Hill, Christopher 22, 32
horse hoe 4
Horse-hoeing Husbandry 4
horsepower 16, 22, 28, 41, 46, 47
Hume, David 2
Hunt, Orator 58–59

Hutton, William 13

Illustrations of Political Economy 103
Imperialism 4, 114, 122
India 9, 44, 114, 115, 116, 118, 122
industrial saboteurs 17, 51, 54, **56–57**
Ireland 2, 6, 98, 124
iron 20–21, **22–23**
iron bridges 43
iron industry 17, **22–23,** 34, 55*m,* 77
　puddling process 23
　"rolling" process 23
iron steamships 44–45
Irwell Valley 42

Jane Eyre 103
Johnson, Paul 15, 38, 65, 75

Kay, John 16
Kay-Shuttleworth, James 101, 103
Keats, John 64, 69
Kemble, Fanny 46
Kilsby tunnel 47
Kipling, Rudyard 120

labor unions 32–34, 53, 78, 97, **118–19,** 124
laissez-faire economics 9, 85, 86, 87, 89, 118
Lamarck, Jean-Baptiste 106
Lancashire, England 9, 76, 93
land enclosures **5–6,** 80, 83, 125
Languedoc Canal 42
Leeds, England 13

popular uprisings **54–59**
population **87–89,** 88
Posthumous Papers of the Pickwick Club 91
Presbyterians 73, 100
Pride and Prejudice 68, 79
Priestley, Joseph 104
prostitution 65, 81, **82–83**
Public Health Act 95
public health system **87–89,** 95
public lectures 69, **104–106**
Pulteney, William 38
Puritan work ethic 73

Quakers 13, 46, 73, 76, 87, 100

Radcliffe, Ann 68
Rainhill Trials 46
railroads 21, 25, *31,* 34, 38, 43– 47, 48, 97, 118
reform movements 4, 32, **53–59,** 61, **71–99, 100–104**
Regency, the 54
Reign of Terror, the 71
Report on the Sanitary Conditions of Large Towns and Populous Districts 95
riots 53, 54, **56–59,** 60, 86
roads 25, **37–41,** 43
Rocket 46, *47*
Romantic Movement, the **63–69**
rotary steam engines 21, 44
Rousseau, Jean-Jacques 63, 64
Rugby School 102
Ruskin, John 112

safety lamps **30–31**
Savery, Thomas 30

Scotland 2, 5, 38, 96, 101
Scott, Walter 47
Shelley, Mary **68–69,** 79
Shelley, Percy 64, 65, 67, 68, 69
sea quadrant 114
Selley W. T. 6
Sepoy Rebellion 115
shipping 41, **44–45,** 48, 76
Shirley 57
slavery 11, 17, 61, 65, **76–78,** 83
slave trade 53, **76–78,** 95
slums 12–13, 53, 86, **87–89,** 90, 93
Smith, Adam **1–3,** 6, 7, 9, 12, 13, 41, 85, 86, 98, 103, 119, 122
Socialism *94*
Society for the Diffusion of Useful Knowledge 103
Society for the Prevention of Cruelty to Children 91
Society of Friends. *See* Quakers
Somerville, Mary 79
South America 17, 76, 107, 109
Southey, Robert 39, 59, 97
Speedenham System **89–90**
"spinning jenny" 9, 51
steam power 23, 113
    engines 11, **18–22, 29–30,** 44
    locomotives **45–46,** 47
    looms 51
    ships 41, **44–45,** 48
    spinning mills 17
    threshing machines 113
steamships 41, **44–45,** 48
steel manufacturing **20–21,** 45, 55*m*
Stephenson, George **45–46**
Stephenson, Robert 46
Stockton and Darlington railway 46
strikes **32–34,** *33,* 53, 93, 97
Suez Canal 118
syphilis 81

tariffs 1, 6, 54, 85, 98
Telford, Thomas **38–39,** 40, 43, 100
Temple, John 26
Tennyson, Alfred 78, 121
Tess of the D'Urbervilles 80
textile industry 8–9, 15, 21, 23, 46, 51, 52, 54, 55*m,* 76–77, 80, 118
Theory of Moral Sentiments, The 2
Thoughts on the Importance of the Manners of the Great to the General Society 74
Tolstoy, Leo 81
Tories 60, 74, 86. *See also* Conservative Party
Toynbee, Arnold 125
trade unions. *See* labor unions
transportation 37–48
Trevelyan, G. M. 80
Trollope, Anthony 79
Tull, Jethro 4, 113
Turner, J. M. W. 64, 65, 68, 69

unions. *See* labor unions
Unitarianism 13

Victoria, queen of England 28, 91, 94, 95, **112–13,** 115, *115,* 119
Vindication of the Rights of Women 78
Volta, Allesandro 106
Voltaire 2
voting rights 87, 124
Voyage of the Beagle, The 109

wage labor 9, 52, 97
Wales 2, 43, 96
War of 1812 53
"water frame" 9, 51
waterwheels 9, 12, 16
Watt, James **18–21,** 29, 44, 100, 101, 104
Watt engine **18–21,** 23
Webb, R. K. 48, 113
Wedgewood, Josiah **10–12,** 34, 41, 43, 104, 109
Wedgewood china 6, **10–12,** *10,* 43
Wesley, John 37, 43, 73
West Indies 76, 77, 114, 122
Whigs 86, 87
White, R. J. 41
Whitely, William 48
Wilberforce, William 74, 76, 77, 78
Wilkinson, John 23, 43
William IV, king of England 86, 94
Wollstonecraft, Mary 68, 78
women
    miners 26, 27, 27, **28–29**
    workers **79–82,** 95
women's rights 68, 75, **78–82,** 124
Wordsworth, Dorothy 64, **65–66**
Wordsworth, William 37, 40, 64, 65, 66, 122
workhouses 90, 91, 93
working conditions **51–53**
World War I 125

Yorkshire, England 57